EDITED BY **MATTHEW PARKER**
AND **EUGENE SEALS**

planting
seeds of
hope

HOW TO REACH
A New Generation
OF AFRICAN AMERICANS
WITH THE GOSPEL

Planting Seeds of Hope

To Tom Skinner,
evangelist, friend, and mentor,
whose investment in emerging leaders
has already produced fruit a hundredfold
in the spirit of 2 Timothy 2:2

CONTENTS

This book offers proactive approaches to evangelism and discipleship in reaching a new generation of African Americans.

The church continues to demonstrate its capacity to facilitate spiritual and social change. Thus, the church and Christian organizations are a natural vehicle for reaching the unreachable. Richard Freeman, a Harvard economist, says, "Churchgoing has a powerful negative effect on socially deviant activity and a positive impact on members' attitudes and behavior. People who go to church are less likely to commit crimes, be unemployed, use drugs or drop out of school."

The objective of this book is to provide how-tos on evangelism for African American pastors and church leaders and to serve as a resource pool for leaders who are focused on evangelism and discipleship.

The vision for the book project comes from my time with Tom Skinner. Skinner's gift of preaching the Gospel to high school and college students encouraged me greatly. The writers are individuals who are communicating the Gospel in imaginative and innovative ways. These successful self-help activities are rooted in the promise that people in the African American community will respond to creative, sensitive, contextualized presentations of the Gospel.

Matthew Parker, President
Institute for Black Family Development

Chapter 1

Ten of the Best Ways Black Men Can Inspire Our Youth

BY JERALD JANUARY, SR.

We hear and read many stories about young African Americans who have no motivation or desire to fulfill their dreams. More disturbing are the countless testimonies of our young who have no dreams at all. Too many of their personalities and actions are borrowed from the latest rap video or violence-laden movie. Too many others have been beaten down by hopelessness before they reach puberty.

While hundreds of illegal immigrants continue to risk their lives daily attempting to live a moment of the American dream, many of this nation's own have decided that it is all worthless. Yes, it is true that many of our young people are on their way to very successful and fulfilling lives. However, we cannot escape the undeniable fact that there are countless others who are running in the opposite direction.

In spite of dramatic decreases in national and local statistics, crime is running rampant among our nation's youth whose moral values have been tossed out the window. Authorities say something has to be done to bring back many of the old family values (the ones that stimulate positive thinking), inspire pride, and motivate young people to pursue productive careers.

In the twenty years or so I have spent working with young people, the one undeniable fact I have experienced is that as a black man I have the power to inspire the next generation to greatness or to failure. It is something that we as men must come to grips with. Often the major variables that differ in the lives of young blacks are the role models or the lack thereof that encouraged them along the way. Some of us seem to feel that it is the responsibility of the government, schools, or some mystical entity to move our children from a place of apathy. It remains a fact, however, that we should be a larger part of what inspires our children, just as many of our forefathers did for us.

Volumes of studies have been amassed that speak of successful models for black youth intervention programs. Many of these, however, seem unattainable to the average brother who initially may be equipped with only a desire to see young folk helped.

With that type of gentleman in mind, I propose a list I have amassed over the years of my own journey. It is simply Ten of the Best Ways Black Men Can Inspire Our Youth.

Talk to Them

As simple as this first offering may seem, I have found that it is one of the biggest issues young people have when it pertains to the older generation. While conducting a rap session with a group of fifty black teens on the south side of Chicago, I asked, "What can we as black men do to help inspire you?" The answer that came from a lovely seventeen-year-old high school senior was quite direct. She said, "Talk to us. We hardly ever have a chance to talk to the men in our community. They always seem too busy or too scared or something." She continued, "It's like when you all make it big we're not important."

One of my greatest joys has come from just getting into a

conversation with the young folks. As a teenager, my brothers and I enjoyed the evenings sitting on the porch with our grandfather, father, and uncle as they talked about everything from sports to the pressures of their jobs. It was special to spend time with the men. Young people of today are no different than we. They seek guidance, friendship, and security in the instruction and inspiration of our words.

Listen to Them

It would seem to follow that if we spend time talking to our young people we would naturally listen as well. Unfortunately, that is not always the case. Many young people maintain no one is willing to listen to them.

My baby brother, André, was your typical teenager from the 'hood. A great-looking kid with a ton of energy and enthusiasm. One day on a trip back to my hometown of Detroit he made an unusual request of me. "Big Brother, I need to talk to you," he said. "Big Brother, I'm scared. These gangs are crazy in Detroit. Can I come and live in Colorado with you during the school year? That way I can be safe and come back to Detroit in the summer."

He looked at me with so much expectation. At the time, I didn't really listen to what he was saying. I gave him a very convenient response: "I'll pray about it."

Months passed, and I hadn't given André's request any thought. One day I felt led to call home from my office. It was then that I was informed that André had been shot and killed. Murdered in the same way he had feared. Shot supposedly by the same menace he asked me to help deliver him from. But I didn't listen.

As we listen to our young people, they will tell us everything we want to know. Listening is a unique part of a relationship that allows us access into the soul of a young person. My last experience with André taught me the importance of listening to our youth.

Practice What You Preach

It is as simple as it sounds. But for some of us it has been difficult to do. Instead, many of us have lived by the motto "Do as I say, not as I do." Maybe that worked when we were growing up, but that is a song this generation will rarely dance to. Our young people spend a great deal of time observing us in our roles as Christians. From the time they are young they watch us as we usher, teach, sing, preach, or simply attend Sunday morning service. They learn from us what is good, bad, righteous, sinful, real, or phony. Some of us have been guilty of teaching this generation some horrible habits.

Like any other young person, the African American youth is more likely to trust and honor the man whose walk matches or exceeds his talk.

Dedicate Time to the Youth of Your Community

Time is a precious commodity. There never seems to be enough of it. One of the best definitions of time I have ever heard is "the measure of eternity." It reminds me of the importance of each new day.

After André died, I spent the majority of my time working with and on behalf of young people. This was actually a reaction to my brother's murder. I almost ruined my marriage trying to be a one-man cure for the ills of young America—a common mistake made by youth workers.

I learned, however, that it was indeed more realistic and honorable to dedicate a portion of time to the youth in my community. I helped form a group called Common Ground. I committed, through my church, to be at our local urban high school each Tuesday of the week for about an hour and a half. There I was given my own classroom where students could come in and discuss all kinds of issues that pertained to their lives.

We started with twelve young black men. Before my four-year commitment was done, we had a group that on occasion numbered as many as fifty students. Many of these youth not only experienced successful educational careers but also received Christ, renewed faith, and/or became active members of local congregations, including ours.

If our nation is ever to be turned around it will take an

army of dedicated black men willing to carve out a designated amount of time and dedicate it to the next generation. There is no substitute for well-invested time!

Share Your Resources

A resource is simply any source of aid or support one can give. Whatever we have to offer that can benefit others can be considered a resource. Yes, money is an excellent example of a resource. The Bible says much about the investment of our "riches."

While it is a fact that the majority of believers in America come to Christ before their twenty-first birthday, our churches usually spend less than 2 percent of the budget on evangelizing or discipling our youth. We commonly wait too late to begin investing our resources in our most valuable commodity.

Money is not the only form of resource. For example, a brother with a van or 4x4 can donate the use of his driving skills and vehicle once a week to a church youth activity or a youth center in the community. Many of our youth have no transportation to activities that will assist them in gaining the knowledge and self-esteem they need to make good choices.

Share Your Knowledge

Our children face some obstacles that many of us have no idea exist. For many of them, their day-to-day experiences cause a level of stress that is almost unbearable. One thirteen-year-old girl admitted to me and her youth group, with tears in her eyes, that "everyday somebody tries to get me to take drugs. Everyday somebody tries to get me to have sex with him. I'm just tired."

Unfortunately, a great number of our youth don't realize that we, too, have had to endure many kinds of pressures. Many of them are surprised when they encounter racial discrimination as well as other obstacles. An adult can teach them they aren't the only ones who have a rough road to travel. They can learn from our knowledge that they can succeed even though sometimes life is not fair.

Bring Your Job to the 'Hood

Because many of our young people come from homes that don't normally afford them the opportunity to see a myriad of careers, it is important that we in the church be intentional about sharing what we do. So often the only thing they see black men doing successfully is playing sports or being part of the entertainment industry. While these careers can be rewarding, your career may be the one that inspires a youngster to aim higher.

I have encouraged youth leaders to offer a time during the youth service or at other gatherings where adults can share with young people what they do for a living. It not only helps them to get to know each other in the church, but also gives young people an opportunity to ask questions they would possibly never be afforded elsewhere.

I have even arranged to take young people to my place of employment to get their feet wet. This allows them to actually see and feel the environment. There are some of us who are able to arrange summer internships for our youth. These types of experiences normally go a long way with young people.

It is possible to become a role model by sharing with young people what you do. By spending time and sharing career opportunities, you may help young African Americans realize they are not trapped in unwanted environments.

Treat Your Lady Like a Lady

I know this option may seem out of place in the context of the others. However, seeing the pitiful way many black men treat their women as well as talk about them is incredible. Many youngsters develop negative attitudes about relationships and their own sexuality by watching adults. Many of our young men and women have no idea how to date or have a meaningful relationship without illicit sex, abusive language, or mistrust. It is up to adults, specifically black men, to be role models in every facet of a young person's life, including the way they allow youngsters to see them function in relationships with their wives, or women in general. Black women, like women of all races, want and deserve to be respected and feel they are safe in the presence of a black man.

Share Your Faith with Them

Over the years of ministering to the needs of the next generation, I have had the blessed opportunity to share many things with young people. My wife and I have on many occasions opened our home to young people who need a place of refuge. It has been a place where they can do their homework after school and have a hot home-cooked dinner. For others, it has been "home" when things at their home were just unbearable.

I have had the opportunity to share with them a ticket to a ball game or a movie. What a joy it has been just to hang out with them and slap a high five after a super slam dunk.

During many conversations over the years, the ultimate question has come up. "Mr. J., you seem to have it all together. How?" Or, "Mr. January, why aren't you bitter about the murders of your family members?" or "Why do you care so much for us?" No matter how tired I get or how busy I am, I never tire of sharing my faith with young people.

I'm not ashamed of where I came from and what the Lord has done in my life. I explain to young people that all that I am and all that I do, even for them, is because of Jesus. I have never had one young person who didn't believe that what God has done in my life is real. Many have come to trust Him for salvation through my testimony. I encourage every man of God, whenever possible, to share his Christian experience with the next generation.

Create Your Own Form of Inspiration

One of the ways black men can inspire our youth is by creating from their own lives a unique form of inspiration. I enjoy following the model of others. However, everybody is different, and those differences have allowed me to do some things that were unique to the situations in which I found myself.

One instance came out of a conversation I was having

with a group of Denver area high school students I had been mentoring. I asked one sixteen-year-old boy where he would choose if he had an opportunity to go anywhere he wanted that summer. His answer stunned me. "I've always wanted to go to Colorado Springs." While Colorado Springs is a nice place, it is only fifty minutes down the road from Denver. I came to find that this young man had never been outside of Denver. His horizons, like those of so many of our children, were limited.

I decided that day that this group of black teens would have an opportunity to have their horizons broadened. I told each one of them that if they made at least a 2.0 during the final semester we were going on an adventure that summer. We were going on a cultural/college tour through parts of America.

My wife, Jerra, and I designed a trip that took eight days and allowed these young people to see colleges, cities, and cultural sites most of them had never before considered.

I called several colleges along the route and worked out special meal plans and sleeping arrangements for us. Most of the colleges were excited to hear that over thirty black youth were interested in looking at their colleges.

The young people had to come up with $100 for the trip and a good report card, and most of them did. We hired a black Christian-owned tour bus company to transport us, and we were on our way. The remainder of the money came from community donations. There were some very generous individual contributions.

We traveled from Denver to Tulsa, toured Oral Roberts University, and were the overnight guests of Pastor Carlton Pearson's Higher Dimension Ministry. The young people appreciated their Sunday service. We went from there to Tuskegee University in Alabama, where the staff at the school treated our young people to a taste of southern hospitality. The historic tours and the opportunity to stay all night on campus highly impacted our kids. We spent three days in Atlanta, Georgia, touring the colleges as well as city sights. Our final stop took us to Indiana and famed Depauw University, where the black student union gave our youth goals to strive for.

The trip, as you can imagine, changed many lives. For those who had already made up their minds to pursue a college degree, they pressed harder. For others who hadn't thought they could do it, they now knew they could. Some of the students now attend schools we visited on the tour.

Probably the greatest miracle of our trip occurred with a young man who wasn't even supposed to go with us. His mother had heard of the tour and petitioned us to take her sixteen-year-old son along. She said he needed this kind of exposure. At the time he was thinking of converting to Islam because of some bad experiences he had had in the Christian church. While on the road with us, he didn't say much at first. However, the young people and adult supervisors treated him the same as everyone else. I received a call from his mother two days after we returned to Denver. She asked me, "What did you do to my son?" I found myself startled. I had no idea what she was talking about. She informed me that on two occasions since he had arrived home he had broken down and started crying. When she asked him what was wrong, his answer was always the same. "This man really loves those kids. I've never seen that kind of love before." As she readied to end our call she said, "I just want to thank you for being a role model for my son."

I have learned over the years that we have countless opportunities to inspire young people around us. The key question is, Are we willing to be that kind of man?

Jerald January, Sr., is president and founder of January Ministries (Colorado Springs, Colo.).

Chapter 2

Caring for and Coping with the First-Year Collegian

BY STEVE HAYES

Childbirth, the first days of school, the first hospital visit, a first step of faith—these are some of the exciting and stressful beginnings most parents experience with their children. Sending a child off to college continues to be one of the more stressful events in a family's life. The causes of this stress are many. However, parents and their child can weather this event successfully with some early preparation.

Over the years I have seen parents drop off their child into a beautiful, scenic, well-maintained campus only to have it become one of the most inhospitable environments a young African American adult could find. Alone, with no friend; frightened, with no guide—only a handbook and a weekend schedule that must be followed—a student looks for the smallest reason to leave that place and return home to family and friends.

However, I have also seen young people who are left on

campus, faces glowing with wonder and excitement, talking with others, seeking to find their initial place at college.

Why the two different faces? Why the two different outlooks? The economic range is broad in both groups, while the intellectual prowess and abilities are similar. The educational backgrounds and experiences are also very much alike. The differences are in the work that both the parents and the children did to prepare for the student to be in this place, the college or university, at this time. Usually good planning, strong decision making, and clear communication between parent and child are the keys to your child's having a successful first-year experience. I hope to share with you much of what parents must do to ensure that their child be ready for that experience.

My Experience

In 1970, when I let my parents know of my intention to go to college, their reactions took me by surprise. My stepfather couldn't understand why a "smart boy" like me would want to waste his time in college when I could go to Washington, D. C., take the civil service exam, and land a good-paying government job. He made it clear that I should not expect any financial support from the family. My mother said she expected me to be the first one to enter college, but she was not sure how she could help me in making the decision about college. My father was excited when I told him what I was planning, but he didn't agree that I should become a teacher. However, he definitely wanted me to get a college education. My grandmother was my strongest supporter. She offered to help me with some of my costs and—more importantly—to pray for me as I made these important choices.

Like everyone else, I heard about the SAT exam and completed the appropriate application form. I checked the boxes that allowed me to waive the fees because I was a "minority" and place my name and scores into a database for colleges to "see" the black students. On my own, I prepared for that exam, then took it and tried to interpret the results.

I received letters from several colleges around the country, but I didn't know that visiting them would have been an important activity. I only visited three schools, each within twenty miles of my home in suburban D.C. I toured them only because I had heard some of my peers talking about visiting schools. Neither my guidance counselor nor my parents suggested looking elsewhere. They each thought the other was doing that job. I did get guided tours in two of the schools, but I walked around the third one alone. I did not visit any of the schools that offered me a minority grant or a scholarship because I looked at the final costs from their brochures and came to the conclusion that I could not afford them.

I chose a local historical black state college with a reputation as a teacher training school. The choice, in large part, was because it was close to home and because I could have my tuition waived if I promised to teach. (I believe we need a similar program today, but that should be addressed in another document.) I commuted because I didn't have the money to afford room and board—I didn't even think about making money for that. After the first month of classes, I spent the next two years trying to get away from that school.

I made poor choices, without knowing better. I had no real help in making my decisions, and the background experiences of my family precluded that good choices would have been made. I believe it is crucial that loving Christian parents do all they can to see that their child, if talented enough, gets into the best college or university available and that he or she excels in that environment.

So here is a word to parents. You know your student. What skills and abilities does this child possess that show you that going to college is the correct decision for the next year? This is a difficult question to ask and answer. We all want to believe that our students can do anything. With their God-given gifts, most will do so much. However, parents must help their child make a good, honest assessment of those gifts, abilities, and skills. Questions need to be asked about the careers that might match those abilities. Questions must be answered about what would aid in your child's continued development of those skills. In the same manner that many families choose in which neighborhood to raise their child, parents should be choosing a college for their child. The child and parent should meet regularly, starting, at the latest, in the student's sophomore year of high school and using the time to ask and seek out the answers to some of these questions.

Questions You Should Ask

Primary questions. Your child should be asking, first, "Why is college the right choice for me?" You can help answer that question by looking at the educational, social, experiential, and spiritual development of your child. Talk out the answers. Write out the answers. Review them in light of new discoveries that are made over the next months or years. Many students leave college because they find they don't belong there. Many times it is not a social issue. They discover that college is not a good fit for them at this time in their lives. Would it have been better to discover that before so many resources were used?

The next question should be, "What are the characteristics of the school I want to attend?" A student should have an idealized view of the college. This question is really the umbrella of many questions: How large or small? In what part of the country (or world) should it be? Who are the people that I could live with? What kinds of facilities do I want or need to be available to me? What focus do I want the school to have? What admissions tests are required? Does the physical atmosphere matter to me? Are the co-curricular activities and athletic activities important? How competitive is the admissions process? How do the faculty interact with the students? How expensive is it? How much financial support does the school provide for its students?

These and more questions concerning that ideal college will be generated during the next one and a half years until your child makes a choice. As the parent, you should encourage active seeking of the answers. That means writing for brochures, visiting campuses and taking tours, talking to representatives of the schools, reading reports and evaluations of the schools, and, especially, talking to current and former students of the schools. This last activity is very important because the students from that school will be able to give a truer picture of the life at that college. They are the ones of whom your child should ask the hardest questions. You should assist in developing those questions.

Secondary questions. These are the personal questions the family must ask. These deal with your resources for college. Discuss with your child how much of the family's income could be made available. A cause for many students to leave college is that there was no real financial support from their families, and they didn't know it until it was too late. Parents should be open and honest with their child. Some families are able to save for their child's college. Some families begin a search for scholarship moneys while the student is still a freshman or sophomore in high school. Others seek assistance from financial aid officers of the college the student chooses, and they get good results. Parents, don't leave this part of the decision making up to your child alone. Eighteen-year-olds have almost no experience in financial matters. Here is where you must take most of the leadership.

Another question that must be answered is, "What are the parents' wishes?" In the United States, we are so individualistic that many times we parents never air what requirements we desire for our child's college education. Let us not forget that we are charged by God to raise up our children. This, however, does not mean that we lord it over our children to the point of causing rebellion. Find the gentle blend of love and discernment that is given to the parent.

Acceptance! Now What?

Your child has written the letters, filled out the applications, and has been accepted to the chosen college! Everyone in the family agrees that the college is the right one for your child. As a parent you have done your best to get a good financial package so that the family can survive this expensive undertaking. In less than six months you will be sending this young adult to live for four years with new people in a new place that will become "home." How do you make the transition a good one and beneficial for all? That is what this final section of the chapter is about: surviving that first semester.

What the parent does. First of all, pray for guidance and peace of heart. Your child is going away, but you should be able to look at this time as God did after the Creation days and say, "It is good." Then you should plan to seek out a body of local believers whom you can ask to look after your child, as you would expect your church members to do for your son or daughter when you were away from them. This may mean a trip to meet with the local minister in a church of your denomination. Many students who continue at a college that is more than five hours away from home do so because they have found roots in the college community. The local church can form strong roots. Also, you might want to see if you have any other connections with people in the area of the college. An old classmate, a business acquaintance, a relative, or even a local member of the service club you are a member of could provide the "touch of home" that might be a life preserver for your college student during the first few weeks or months of school.

You will also want to establish with your child when and how your communications will develop. Will there be letters every day or once a week? Will there be unlimited telephone calls? Is E-mail an option? (Many colleges are giving students E-mail accounts when they register for classes.) This gives some students letters from home with the speed of a telephone call. Having regular communication is a very stabilizing factor in a first-year student's life. If you write, don't forget to send stamps to your child. Then you will receive letters, too.

This is the time to develop how your child will receive and use the funds for this first semester. Will there be a bank account? Will the money be in a school account? Try to stay away from credit cards, but a money access card could work like a checking account. Make that decision early and practice it before the first day of classes.

Finally, I encourage you to pray for your child each day.

The "fiery darts of the evil one" can and will be flung into the pathways of our children as they leave our homes. Even at a Christian college, we must seek the care of the Holy Spirit to guide and direct them.

What the student does. As with the parent, the student should rejoice and pray! You are beginning another level of training, and this is on your own. Or at least it might feel that way. You are encouraged to initiate correspondences with a few important people. First, your roommate(s). From the student life office of your school, find the name(s) of those who will be living with you. Write to them and introduce yourself. Include a photo that shows who you are. A prom or graduation picture may not be the best. This person will be the one who sees you at your worst and best. If the college is not a historical black college, you may be living with someone who will have a lot of questions about living with a black person. You can get some of those awkward questions answered with a few phone calls before school starts. Discuss each other's likes and dislikes concerning living situations: music, television shows, books, foods, colors, styles. Try to go into the dorm living situation with a sense of peace and excitement.

Next, you will want to continue your contact with the admissions counselor with whom you met upon visiting the college. Let that person know that you expect some further interaction after you have arrived. Then you will know at least one person when you arrive on campus.

An office to contact before and after you arrive, especially if you attend a school where blacks are in the minority, is the student minority affairs office. This is a place where you should find support, care, and guidance during each of your years in college. The persons in this office may be able to give you opportunities to develop your leadership skills that might not be available to you otherwise just because of the large numbers of others on campus. Get them to know you early in your college career.

The other two persons with whom you should attempt to build relationships are your academic advisor, who will help you to direct your college career, and a faculty member from the department in which you have your major. From your visit you should have asked who the good professors are—the ones who would be interested in you and what you want to do. I suggest you choose one and write a letter to her or him. Announce your plan to attend that college and ask for a time when you two could meet, perhaps for a snack during the first week of school. A student who establishes a positive professional relationship with a faculty member, especially in a mentoring capacity, has a more positive first semester than those who do not. Remember, professors are there because of the students. They want to interact with you.

All colleges are not the same. Look for the best fit for you. Perhaps a large university is not for you. Maybe a small Christian liberal arts college, or a Bible college, or even a community college would be better.

God wants you to be complete. When you are making these decisions, look to your parents, whom God has given to you, for assistance and guidance.

If you attend a school where you are in the minority, don't believe that everyone who is not like you is against you. *There are good people in every place.*

Whether you are in a Christian or a secular college/university, seek out a group of Christians with whom you can build strong ties. We need to be accountable to someone for our walk. Continue in your weekly worship and fellowship.

Like Moses, or even our Lord Jesus, this is a wilderness time—a time for you to learn more of who you are and what God has planned for you to do. This is an academic time full of good non-academic activities. Be careful to know when each should have a priority.

Even though you are away from your church family, don't forget them. They are praying for you and they are interested in your life. Write to the church regularly. They will either read your letter aloud or place it on a bulletin board for all to read. Let them know what is going on with you. They care for you.

What the church does. With the pastor at the lead,

before the students leave for college, the local body should gather to commit these souls to the Lord for the new work that will be done in their lives. I have always liked the dedication service my church participates in at the end of the summer. This lets the students know that we are praying for them and that they are being held accountable for their work and lives even though they are away. Members should also be available to keep in touch with the students, especially first-year students.

A letter or telephone call, just to let them know that they are missed, is encouraged. Keeping our young adults connected to the church, even at long distances, is vital to keeping the church stable and growing. These are our future leaders. We want to bring them home so that they can continue that "good work."

Our children seem to have so much to look forward to. We must give them the opportunities that they need to be successful. It is my hope that in following these suggestions, those who choose to attend college will do so with peace and assurance.

Steve Hayes is assistant professor of education at Messiah College (Grantham, Pa.).

Chapter 3

Who Can Work with Our Youth?

BY RUSSELL KNIGHT

Many African American youth no longer look to the church, the school, or the family as the center of their lives. Parents can no longer count on the church to have the answers on how to reach, teach, and train this lost generation of young people.

While in the military, I was taught to calibrate my rifle using the following method. First, fire several rounds of ammo at the target. Then, check to see if you are hitting the target too far left, too far right, or dead center. If, when you aim dead center, you consistently hit right or left of the target, overcompensate away from center in the opposite direction as indicated on your target. Finally, shoot another round of ammo to test the theory. You should now be hitting dead center.

At some point, while the church was aiming at African American youth, things changed. In this case, the target remained the same, but the conditions and the environment shifted. Unfortunately, the church has not recalibrated in order to ensure that it is hitting the new target dead center. We are still aiming at the target of the fifties, sixties, or seventies. During those eras the target was not moving as much as it is today. The modern target is far more hazy than in the past.

The environment into which today's urban child is born is vastly different from the one into which I was born. More urban kids are born without the benefit of having two parents in the home and are destined to live in poverty during their formative years, if not for their entire lives. Many live in drug- and alcohol-infested communities and are raised in neighborhoods where violence is a way of life. Their concept of morality centers around the idea of not getting caught. Many do not expect to live until they are grown. Fewer young people than ever before make any connection with God, Jesus, the church, or the Bible.

Growing up barely able to read and without the realization that the world is larger, more competitive, and less accepting than just their neighborhood, many live in isolation from other races and ethnic groups. Furthermore, many possess low self-esteem. Recognizing the multifaceted deficits that characterize many youth, Chicago Urban Reconciliation Enterprise (CURE) developed a rite-of-passage experience for urban youth. We have seen good success in using this experience to address critical developmental issues. The program opens up avenues of communication whereby we may talk about spiritual things as well.

Helping Our Youth Develop Self-Esteem: A Three-Month Rite-of-Passage Experience

Have each student select a hobby that will be reported on weekly to the group. This helps students with consistency, achievement, and the idea of finishing what they start.

Discuss "What's in a Name?" and why it is important to respect one's name. Use Bible characters such as Abraham or Peter, and talk about how slaves acquired their names.

Explore the historic evidence for Africa as the "cradle of

civilization." Discuss other views.

Compare the real map (called the Peters' Map) and the traditional map. Discuss why the former is better.

Have students write a letter to their alderman, mayor, governor, or another official to gain firsthand research information on a topic for a research paper or report.

Have students write a research paper relating to their regular studies (science, language, social studies).

Have students prepare an oral presentation about an African American who has made a major contribution in areas such as science, politics, or religion. Avoid the areas of sports and entertainment.

Take a field trip to a science museum and divide the group into smaller groups to report on what they learned.

Require students to engage in an approved service project where they do something for others without getting any reward. They must also faithfully perform two tasks at home over the duration of this group experiment.

Require students to open savings accounts. Reward those who add to their accounts during the experiment.

Have students find blacks in the ancient world. Then have them find blacks in the Bible and in the genealogy of Jesus. Discuss what this proves.

Require each student to prepare one meal each month for his or her family.

Require each student to attend church at least twice each month.

Invite to speak to the group a role model who had to overcome great odds in order to succeed.

End the program with a graduation and awards dinner. Encourage students to invite parents and peers.

Alive at Twenty-Five

Tragically, more and more urban kids don't even plan on being alive at twenty-five. Death is a common occurrence; and its impact is trivialized by Hollywood, causing many to vacillate between fantasy and reality.

Historically, the church impacted our communities in a

positive way. Now it, too, must change or find itself powerless in dealing with today's changing youth culture. We can no longer insist that all of our programmatic offerings originate within the four walls of our church building. It now is necessary to transition young people into the church through creative programs that might have to start on their own turf. We must find novel ways of giving young people the benefits of church outside the four walls. Some of our youth require conditioning to function in a church environment, and our churches need to be conditioned to receive uncharted youth. We cannot assume that either is prepared for the other.

As a youth worker in my earlier days, it was not necessary for me to be a social worker, conflict manager, job counselor, crisis counselor, substitute parent, or policeman. Every now and then I was called on to assist a young person in some area of life that was the focus of his or her adolescent struggle. Today's urban youth worker must be all of these and more every day. Urban youth in previous generations were exposed to a system of values that was taught not only at home, but reinforced by the extended family, friends, neighbors, teachers, coaches, employers, and preachers. Not only has the process broken down at the home level, but it appears that all of the backup systems have failed also. This has left our youth morally, spiritually, and biblically bankrupt.

In the past, the church was right on target in its ability to assist the community in reaching out to those under twenty-five. Not long ago the church was able to reach most youth through the programs offered within its four walls. Each church reached its share of unreached youth because eventually someone (perhaps a grandmother) would bring the young person to the church even when the parents had forsaken the child's religious upbringing. Tragically, with several generations of parents and grandparents being disconnected from church, today's urban young person actually might reach adulthood without ever having personally attended church.

Youth workers no longer fit any preordained mold. They may be college age, single or married, male or female, middle-aged, or senior citizen. In fact, the church would be wise to insure that a diverse group of youth workers makes up the team.

Those seeking to be successful in today's urban youth culture must understand that urban youth (including African Americans) draw most of their values from their music and from movies, videos, and television. It would appear that today's youth worker needs degrees in language and communications and must also function as a referral service when it comes to helping youth with problem solving.

Counseling African American Students in Crisis

Encourage students in crisis to talk about themselves, their families, and their experiences. This is a good way to determine the students' belief systems. The counselor should be vulnerable by sharing about himself.

Don't count on observation of the students' behavior alone to define the students. Ask questions.

Allow students to talk about the celebration of holidays and their religious experiences. This is useful in group sessions.

Encourage students to talk about their family network (grandparents, aunts, uncles, cousins, nieces, nephews). Often they have godparents and substitute relations in their network.

Don't be afraid to give specific, explicit answers and advice. They often understand this as a sign of genuine caring.

Allow students to evaluate you and tell you whether they think you can help them.

Encourage students to express their concerns in their own words. They may tend to use language that is natural for them, but raw for you. Deal with the language problem separately.

Make the connection between the students' view of their own behavior and the views of the "significant other" adults in their lives (parents, guardians, family members, or church members).

Recognize the importance of music, dance, and art as modes of communicating their values, culture, and heritage.

You might get them to write about a certain hero or draw a picture of the self they project into the future.

Visit the home of each student. Much will become clear about the student as a result of your witnessing his or her "context." Parents, though suspicious at first, need eventually to see you as a friend who wants to help them with the difficult task of parenting.

Today's urban youth worker must be prepared to periodically move some kids right into his or her own home in order to guarantee that at least some of our youth are exposed to positive things for longer periods of time than for the usual one-hour youth meeting hosted by our churches. He or she must assist parents in the difficult task of raising teenagers and enlist parents as partners in ministry.

Today's urban youth worker must be prepared to teach formally. He or she must also be able to teach informally through trusting relationships. Along with the Bible, the youth worker must teach the values—the good things that everyone says "all parents" teach their kids at home. Such things as manners, respect, honesty, and hard work have to be taught alongside reading, writing, and math. Added to this list are such topics as how the systems work that affect their lives (such as nations, countries, states, cities, neighborhoods, families, schools, and corporations). Society cannot expect mothers who started having children at fourteen to have learned how to instruct their own kids in the difficult area of sexuality or even how to deal with the opposite sex.

Urban youth workers who give their lives to African American youth must be able to connect the history and culture of those they attempt to reach with their present dilemma as articulated in Scripture. They must be ready to interpret youth to parents, thereby helping parents and other adults understand this generation of teenagers.

Finally, but most important, today's youth worker who ministers in the midst of African American youth must love this lost generation and see them as precious jewels to be protected and fruit to be cultivated and harvested. More than ever, today's youth worker must experience ongoing training in order to deal with this ever-changing treasure. Today, as in the past, churches must ask for volunteers to work with today's youth. Only a handful of African American churches are able to afford paid youth workers, but churches must find ways of providing volunteers with the essential training required by those who give their lives to the complex task of reaching and saving a generation that is considered endangered by many.

Russell Knight is president and founder of Chicago Urban Reconciliation Enterprise.

Related Reading

Freeman, Joel A., Don B. Griffin, and Eugene Seals (Ed.). (1997). *Return to Glory: The Powerful Stirring of The Black Man*. Woodbury, New Jersey: Renaissance Productions.

Knight, Russell. (1993). *Take 5: Urban Youth Workers Training Manual*. Chicago: Chicago Urban Reconciliation Enterprise.

McKissic, William Dwight, Sr., and Anthony T. Evans. (1994). *Beyond Roots II: If Anybody Ask You Who I Am: A Deeper Look at Blacks in the Bible*. Wenonah, New Jersey: Renaissance Productions.

Nix, Sheldon D., and Eugene Seals (Ed.). (1996). *Becoming Effective Fathers and Mentors*. Colorado Springs, Colo.: Cook.

———. *Let the Journey Begin*. Colorado Springs, Colo.: Cook.

———. *Let the Journey Begin—Boy's Activity Book*. Colorado Springs, Colo.: Cook.

Ware, A. Charles, and Eugene Seals (Ed.). (1998). *Prejudice and the People of God: Reconciliation Rooted in Redemption Guided by Revelation*. Indianapolis: Baptist Bible College of Indianapolis.

Chapter 4

Reaching and Nurturing African American Youth

BY REV. MICHAEL THOMAS WESTBROOK

Therefore go and make disciples of all nations, baptizing them in the name of the Father and of the Son and of the Holy Spirit, and teaching them to obey everything I have commanded you. And surely I will be with you always, to the very end of the age" (Matthew 28:19–20 NIV). "And he must needs go through Samaria" (John 4:4).

These are the commands of Scripture and the heart of youth ministry. With all the news coming out in the media about our youth, even though somewhat depressing, there is no greater challenge for the church than to go out and reclaim our young people.

In addition, we have to do it with all the urgency we can muster. The kind of fervor I'm advocating can be found in the Gospels in the story of the paralytic. Just as those four men did not let anything stop them from bringing their paralyzed friend to the feet of Jesus, we, too, should have that desire for our young people who are caught in the negative forces of society.

This chapter recounts one couple's attempt to bring young people to the feet of Jesus. It is my attempt, through my story, to prayerfully give you some tools to use in your own situation. It is my prayer that all of it applies to your situation. If not, I give you what my mentor and Bible instructor would say: "Eat the meat, and spit out the bones."

When I was first approached by Young Life to pioneer a new ministry in the city of Newark, New Jersey, I must admit that I didn't greet the news with overwhelming enthusiasm. Newark at that time in the mid-1980s was listed as the poorest city in the United States. It had all the problems that come with being the largest city in a state—a mass exodus of the middle class and various other social and fiscal ills that often plague big cities. To reinforce all of that, PBS televised a Bill Moyers documentary that underscored the problems of Newark.

Driving Newark

Having spent my childhood in Newark and growing up in and around the city, it wasn't those problems that concerned me. In fact, when I started with Young Life, I was living in a smaller city close by that was facing problems similar to those in Newark, albeit on a smaller scale. Working with young people in the church and in that city, I was already dealing with problems associated with the city.

When I was asked to start a youth outreach ministry in Newark, I was hesitant, not because of the challenge, but because I wondered if there was a need for me to go there. Having been a minister and a Christian education director in the local church in which I had grown up, I knew that Newark was one of the most "churched" cities in the country. In a place where so many churches resided, my continuous prayer to God as I began to drive through the streets was, "Is there a need?"

As I drove, I saw young people on street corners—some standing idle, others dealing drugs. Whether it was day or night, I saw lots of young people out on the streets. God visibly answered my prayers as I drove one night. I saw a group of young people sitting idly on the steps of a large church, while behind them, across the front of the building, was a tall chain-linked fence. As I processed that scene, the Lord seemed to speak to me and say, "That is why your ministry is needed; the children can't get into My house."

Incarnational Approach

John 4 is one of my favorite passages. John 4:4 records, "Now [Jesus] had to go through Samaria" (NIV). Anyone who knows anything about historic Jewish-Samaritan relations can appreciate the significance of that statement. Just as Jesus purposed Himself to go through Samaria, I made up my mind to go where young people congregated. I became visible on basketball courts and various streets in my target community. After I had made the decision to fulfill God's call for me to come to Newark, my wife, Maria, and I transferred our membership to a church in our new community.

We felt that not only did we need to live in the community, we needed to be visible in worship there also. St. John Unified Freewill Baptist Church became our base of membership and operation. The church and its pastor, Bishop Curtis D. Gilmore, provided immediate credibility with the community. We in turn brought to the church our experience as youth ministers.

Once school started, our pastor enhanced our credibility even more by personally taking me to the high schools located in our community and introducing me to the principals. This was important, for even though I wasn't going to work directly in the high schools, I wanted to have a presence around the schools and the sporting events. The pastor's introduction identified me as a minister in the community and as someone who cared for the well-being of young people. With his introduction, I avoided being looked on with suspicion or being labeled as a potential predator or threat to the young people.

Territorial Survey

While in the initial stages of making contact with young people, I began to fulfill one of my other goals, which was to avoid duplicating what was already in existence. This involved doing the community research of identifying and visiting churches, youth-serving agencies, and recreation centers to get an idea if the young people were being served and their needs being met. I discovered at that time that many of the groups I visited were then focusing on young children. Since we were working with adolescents as our target group, the field was wide open. It was disheartening to see that a large portion of the teenage population had little in the way of ministry or services geared directly to them.

Meeting the Need

Our community research indicated that there was a need for recreation and a safe place for young people to gather to learn to be sociable with one another. After surveying the land, my wife and I decided on a course of action. My visibility in the community had begun to pay off. I was at the stage where I had won friends and maybe quite possibly influenced people. After spending time hanging out at one young man's porch around the corner from the church, I discovered I had hit on the mother lode of contact. This was a place where young people congregated. From there, I was asked along on backyard basketball games.

This was a significant gain for me. Even though I had wrestled from junior high to college and was built like a big offensive lineman for the Dallas Cowboys, my basketball skills were not much to brag about. I was no Michael Jordan. I wasn't even Frank Jordan, whoever he is. I soon discovered in the world of backyard basketball—with its potholes, parked cars, mounds of dirt, bumpy surfaces, and crooked basketball rims—that your skill or lack thereof didn't matter. Just as long as you could maneuver between the garden and the parked car, avoid the pothole, and release your shot at the right angle to make it into the bent rim, you were OK. My math teacher had been right. I could use geometry in the real world!

After several outings of backyard basketball, I suggested that we form a team. After securing some unused gym space in another church, we started our team. That was the beginning of our basketball ministry in 1986. It has since been passed on to more capable hands.

While I worked on basketball, my wife discovered some unused sewing machines at one of the recreation centers. These machines provided an opportunity to fulfill another goal we had established—serving and giving ourselves away to our community. Having won awards in high school for being an excellent seamstress, Maria volunteered to run sewing classes at the recreation center. This enabled her to build some close relationships with the young ladies. The Lord provided this opportunity at the right time, since the young ladies didn't quite hang out like the guys did, and we had been looking for and praying about ways we could reach them.

As we were doing these two activities, we still maintained the church as a base. Involving ourselves in the church's scout troop allowed us to reach more young people in the community and to bring some new youth into the church. In addition to scouting, we started a youth night during which we had a rap session and occasionally showed a Christian film. Having established a relationship with the local Christian film distributor, I was able to call on him to help steer me to the films that were relevant to the young people I was working with. Our pastor, recognizing our need for space, gave us use of four small rooms upstairs in the church. One of the deacons, whose daughter had been coming out to the youth night activities, volunteered materials, paint, and workers to fix up the space.

Having been involved in the ministry for about a year at this point, we finally were able to fulfill the goal of providing a safe place where kids could gather. With four small rooms (one of which was used as an office), a donated Ping-Pong table, and a couch, we started a nightly teen drop-in center. With the opening of the center, attendance began to explode.

Proclaiming the Gospel

Even with all the activities I have mentioned up to this point, I recognized what I was called to do. I knew I wasn't a recreation leader or a social worker. I was a minister whose ultimate goal was to lift up the name of Jesus Christ before young people. What these other activities had done was to give us an opportunity to build relationships with these young people. Our relationships had earned us the right to be heard. It had given us a platform from which we could communicate the Gospel. All during this time the young people, parents, and everyone else were well aware that I was a minister active in a local church and that I ran an outreach ministry called Young Life in partnership with the local church. All during this time, we counseled with and witnessed to the young people about Jesus Christ. We also tried to live out the Gospel before them as best as we could.

Anyone who has worked in urban youth ministry for any number of years knows that only limited amounts of resource materials have been available. The material available was primarily Sunday school curriculum. That situation has changed somewhat through efforts of the editors of this book and a few others. In the early days of this outreach ministry, the only material available was geared toward white suburban church youth groups. It was good for the context for which it was designed, but for the young people I was working with, most of it didn't apply. So I followed the philosophy of my Bible school teacher and mentor and developed what I needed. It was important for our youth to have materials that were contextualized, that is, took their life context seriously.

At one time in the African American community the church itself held such a prominent place in the lives of family members that on Sunday mornings the streets were deserted because everyone went to church. Even if you weren't a regular attendee you still had a reverence for the Lord's Day. There has grown up in our midst, however, a generation of young people who have not been exposed to church and find it hard to revere what the community once held in reverence. Yet, in these young people there is a hunger and desire for the things of God.

Wednesday night at the church was Bible study and prayer meeting night, so it became Bible study night at the drop-in center also. As the young people began to ask questions about the things of God, the Bible study became more evangelistic. It began to take on the theme of "God's view on . . ." Some themes used were "God's view on dating," "God's view on sex," and "God's view on racism." When we started that series, we began to get packed out every Wednesday night. Whenever a new family joined or was visiting the church, the members sent the teens upstairs to us.

We eventually added a Bible club format to our proclamation. This consisted of some songs and a brief message, usually given by me on some passage of Scripture. "Club," as we call it, was made easier once we went to camp, taking the young people away from their usual distractions.

What separates our ministry from social service agencies and youth agencies, in general, is that we lift up the name of Jesus! When Jesus Christ is lifted up to all the earth, He will draw all men, women, boys, and girls to Himself.

Pouring Your Life In

Once we have the attention of young people, we must not make the mistake of sitting back and gloating over our success. We must realize that our job is just beginning. Matthew 28:19–20 mandates in the words of Christ that we are to make disciples.

When our Lord and Master, Jesus Christ, went about disciple-making, He invested His time, wisdom, and knowledge in the disciples' lives. Jesus' discipleship training program consisted of three years of demonstration, on-the-job training, and supervised internship. While traveling the countryside, Jesus would use situations and teachable moments to help His disciples fully grasp His mission and theirs. At the conclusion of that time, with the undergirding of the Holy Spirit, the disciples were ready to stand on their own. In a sense, Jesus poured His life into each of their individual lives.

To make a lasting impression on the young lives God has

entrusted to our care, we have to pour our lives into theirs. What I'm advocating is more than a program. It is allowing young people to become a part of your life. For example, a simple trip to the bank to make some transactions can turn into a lesson on thrift, conducting business, care and use of a checking/savings account, and the like. All of this can be learned as the young person observes you conducting your business and as you use teachable moments to show them how to set up their own accounts. The possibilities are endless. A trip to the grocery store can be a lesson on food selection, budgeting, comparison shopping, and more. As I began to go deeper with young people, I let them get involved in aspects of my life. I, in turn, was becoming involved in their lives.

I took an interest in the things of their world—school, sporting events, plays, and so forth. Much of what is learned by young people is "caught" more than formally taught. They learn through observation and, finally, implementation. While observing other communities and people groups, I noticed that whether it was the suburban country club or the little corner convenience store run by newly arrived immigrants, they always included young people to observe while they participated in their normal activities. It is important as African American people to pour our lives into our young people as well.

A brief word of caution. Please make sure that you save parts of your life for your family and yourself when appropriate. It is very easy in this relational style of ministry to get so caught up in ministry that you neglect time with your family and the time you need for your own personal development.

Supporting Parents

Children are God's gift to parents. God has ordained parents to be the primary caregivers and providers for their children. Our history in America has caused the African American family to develop and adopt survival strategies in order to withstand the pressure from outside forces. One with which we are all familiar is the concept of the extended family.

Growing up in a single-parent household, my mother welcomed the positive intervention of other people, especially men, in my life. As a minister to young people, I know that it is my role to help support and strengthen the role of the parents of the youth in my care. Since our ministry is outreach in nature, and since many of the parents themselves may not have a relationship with Christ, I sometimes end up ministering to the whole family. This ministry might consist of just visiting to give out information, or it might mean intervening in a crisis and witnessing to the love of Jesus Christ. In my own case, it has also meant that my wife and I took a young man into our home at the death of his mother.

The role of the family is such an important one in our community. That is why I believe God has called the church—and His people individually—to help bring about restoration where there has been fragmentation.

Leadership Recruitment and Development

I almost entitled this subheading "No More Lone Rangers," but even the Lone Ranger has Tonto. As you have read through this chapter, you could have gotten the impression that I did everything by myself. Not so. Even though God initially gave me the vision, one of my early goals was to raise up community-based leadership.

At various stages of this chapter, you have read the many times in which I included my wife, Maria, in the text. In Maria, God has given me a partner for life and a partner in ministry. She is one who shares both the vision and the call to the ministry, and we have a mutual desire to see young people reached for the kingdom.

As a young African American, spending her teenage years near Los Angeles in the neighboring cities of Compton and Lynwood, California, with gang violence and youth problems of every type raging all around her, Maria was able to navigate through those rough situations with the help of an outreach ministry to young people. A preacher from Detroit, Michigan, who had been called by God to go to Compton, reached out to her and to other young people, nurturing their faith in Christ and eventually planting a church that created a church home for them.

Even with such a strong partner as Maria, we still needed to build a team of people who would come alongside the young people with us. Scripture teaches us that the harvest is plentiful, but the laborers are few, and that we are supposed to pray to the Lord of the harvest to send laborers. In seeking out leaders, we first realized we needed to pray. We also were very selective. Not everyone has the tools, gifts, and calling to work with young people. We had to choose people who had a relationship with Christ, were spiritually mature, and were in agreement with the vision we had for reaching young people. Because of those requirements, not many people were beating down our door. A few did come along eventually to help with some specific things.

The small trickle of adult response made us double our efforts in training young people as leaders themselves. In our goal to make them into disciples, we also had to teach them and allow them to lead their peers.

The young people who showed a natural gift for leading their peers were set apart and trained as leaders. Reproduction is an important part of discipleship. First we had to challenge our young people to develop a desire to do that. The next step was training them in what to do. The same principles we used elsewhere in our ministry—observation, experimentation, and implementation—we used here, as well. Of the eight staff and twenty volunteers we currently have, a large portion have been raised up through our ministry.

Ministry of Camping

Camping can be a life-changing experience for young people. The opportunity to take young people away from their regular routine has always been a large part of this ministry. My participation in Boy Scouts throughout my school years has given me a love for camping and the great outdoors. Our camping program has consisted of tents and cabins at a Boy Scout campground, weekend retreats at denominational camps and retreat centers, and summer and school-year camping at Young Life camps (which are more like resorts) geared for young people. The benefits of a regular camping ministry are many:

- Getting young people away from their surroundings
- Opportunity to model your faith
- Experiencing God's beauty in His creation
- Being with other young people
- The Word of God impacting their lives through corporate worship

Cost is always a factor in this kind of effort. We have raised money through direct appeal letters, church offerings, church budgets, and individual church members sponsoring all or part of the cost. Whatever method or combination is used, the benefits far outweigh the cost.

In addition to the Young Life outreach and discipleship camps that we are a part of, we also sponsor a Teen Impact Weekend Camp. This consists of young people and their leaders affiliated with churches throughout New Jersey. The weekend includes speakers, seminars, and recreation with the objective of teaching young people to reach out to their peers with the Gospel of Jesus Christ.

Assimilation

The ultimate goal of any outreach ministry should be to incorporate the young people into the local body of believers. This ministry is no exception. I want young people to become saved and have the full experience of being involved in the local church.

I recently had the opportunity to speak to the senior citizens' group at my home church, Fountain Baptist Church of Summit, New Jersey. Included in the group were former Sunday school teachers, choir directors, and various others who were instrumental in keeping me on the straight and narrow path. I had the chance to thank them and tell them that they were living testimonies of the faithfulness of God.

Many young people in our communities are missing out on the intergenerational experience of a local church body. Whenever a crisis or an obstacle came up when I was a child, the church would gather together and have a prayer meeting. One of the mothers of the church would stand up and lead the congregation in one of those old songs of Zion.

The challenges of assimilation rest mostly on the local body of believers. Is your church prepared to accept young people with little or no church background, maybe even from a different economic status? Is your church prepared to receive young people whose styles of dress and speech are different?

I was approached by a church member one time who asked me if I was aware of what kinds of kids were hanging out at the drop-in center. At the time, there were a young lady who was pregnant, some high school guys who were forming a step team, some guys who looked like drug dealers (and were), and various other individuals. I replied to her by saying, "What better place for them to be! When they are in front of my face, they're not trying to get in someone else's negatively." As long as drug dealers follow the rules, which include no recruiting and no dealing, why not have them in a place where they can hear the life-changing Word of God?

The African proverb we sometimes overuse, "It takes a whole village to raise a child," has some meaning for the local church. What better concept of a village than the local church, where members of the body have responsibility for each of the youth in its care?

As the local church accepts the role of being the village, it also becomes a lighthouse in the community. One way you know you are getting through is when tragedy strikes—to whom do they turn? Two instances come to my mind that let me know we had started turning the corner.

The first involved a young lady who had been tragically shot to death. She was one of the first young ladies in Maria's sewing class. The church opened its doors and had the funeral there, with the pastor preaching and presiding. Most of the high school turned out that day.

The other incident involved a young man with whom I had a strong relationship. His mother had collapsed on their porch, in his arms. Failing to revive her, he called 911. With no help coming soon, this young man ran four long blocks to the church, with which he had begun a relationship. There he encountered the pastor and two of the deacons. They went back to the house with him to offer their help. Sadly, the mother did end up passing away. Again, the church opened its doors and held the funeral there.

I remember my pastor saying, as we were making the arrangements, "Even though his mother isn't a member of our church, *he is one of ours.*"

Rev. Michael Thomas Westbrook is director of Multi-ethnic Urban of Young Life (Newark, N.J.).

Chapter 5

Connecting with Today's Youth: It's a Family Affair

BY JAMES WHITE

After fourteen years of full-time youth ministry with Campus Crusade for Christ, I am just beginning to understand a key point. The challenges of youth ministry are not just with the youth. Yes, it is difficult speaking to today's youth. They are very different from the youth of just five years ago. They are ever changing at a rapid pace. It is not easy to stand in front of high school students and keep their attention. It is not easy to make a connection with them.

The *real* challenge—the real success of youth ministry after all these years—is getting parents to understand how to connect with and communicate with African American youth. When it comes to youth ministry, we can come up with all the strategies we want but may not succeed when it comes to results. It is very similar to the educational process. You can have the best school and the best teachers, but without parents being connected with their children, all is in vain. The key to youth ministry goes beyond just having a youth pastor or youth worker. The key to youth ministry as we go into the new millennium is to help parents understand how to connect with youth.

I have a lot of growing to do in the area of connecting with my own three children. Developing African American youth really is a family affair. There are three elements that are important with African American youth—especially when it comes to parents connecting with their youth:

1. Know your child.
2. Grow with your child.
3. Show your child.

Know Your Child

This is one of the most difficult things to do today. Sometimes we live under the illusion that there is a tremendous generation gap between our youth and ourselves. It is easy after we reach the age of thirty and begin moving into our forties to develop amnesia about what we were like when we were teens. But if we look closely at ourselves, we can know our kids.

How do you know your child? First, *know your child's personality*. How would you describe your own personality when you were a teenager? We have a generation today that feels like they are invincible. This is amazing, and there are a variety of reasons for this attitude. There is a feeling that death will not happen. It is surprising how youth today respond to authority—even to a policeman who has a gun to their heads. They could easily say, "Go ahead and pull the trigger," because of this idea of invincibility. That is why the messages of safe sex and waiting until marriage have fallen upon deaf ears with youth.

The personalities of our children fall into two main categories—introverts and extroverts. Introverts are the kids who usually stay to themselves. They are energized by being by themselves. Introverts are the kids who would rather be at their Nintendo, Play Station, or whatever the current most popular video game might be, than with people. They would rather be locked away in their room than deal with people. Sometimes parents misunderstand that as being antisocial, but usually it is just the personality of their kids.

Some kids are extroverts. Extroverts are usually noisy, talkative, driven to be around people and "in the know."

So when it comes to knowing our children, the first thing we have to consider is personal makeup: what are they like and what is their personality?

Second, *what are your child's personal interests?* This is where we have allowed there to be such a chasm, such a distance, between our children and us. We do not understand their personal interests. When it comes to our children's personal interests, five elements influence them greatly: television, music, movies, a sedentary lifestyle, and image.

Television. It has been said over and over again that they are a TV generation, but the same is true for many of us who grew up in the eighties. We, too, are a TV generation. We grew up with such situation comedies as *Good Times*, *The Jeffersons*, *Been There and Back*, *What's Happening*, and *Sanford and Son*. It is not really different with this generation. We cut our wisdom teeth with *Green Acres* and *Petticoat Junction*. We did not have BET (Black Entertainment Television); but we did have those afternoon dance shows, *American Bandstand* and *Soul Train*. We grew up with some of the same elements this generation has.

TV is a major influence for this generation. It is not as though there is one segment of TV that is off limits for today's youth. Every aspect of TV influences today's youth. Even with the ratings and warning labels, you still have a number of teens who are very much into soap operas. And, with the invention of the VCR, many kids do not miss their favorite soap operas, even if they are televised during school hours. Shows that are directed to African American youth have become popular.

When we were growing up in the eighties and early nineties, we were given one choice, perhaps the *Cosby Show*.

Now there are a host of programs to choose from on practically every network from Fox to UPN because television executives realize there is a strong market of African American viewers into which they can tap. To capture that market, they provide sitcoms like *Living Single*, *In the House*, and *Malcolm and Eddie*, not to mention talk shows like *Vi*, *Keenan and Ivory Wayans*, and even some of your other talk shows, like *Ricki Lake* and *Jerry Springer*. Teens are not so much into Oprah because she attracts more of an adult audience. The more sensational, the better for today's teens. A popular show like *Keenan and Ivory Wayans* has sexual innuendo all throughout.

Today's television programs are targeted at today's youth. If we are going to know our youth—if you are going to know your child—you have got to know what they are watching on television.

Music. Music is a very big influence today. It always has been. When it comes to dealing with African American youth there is one word you must understand. It is a term that has been around for a while: *hip hop.*

Hip hop did not start in the nineties. It started back in the eighties, and many would even say before that. The early fathers of hip hop would be names like Cool Kurt and African Bam Bota. Knowledge of the reasons hip hop came by its name is important if you are going to understand your child. Cool Kurt and other deejays decided they were going to have two turntables and make a special sound, a special music, by hopping from one turntable to the next. Thus, hip hop was born. As critical as we want to be of hip hop, it is an amazing musical expression. If we want to know our children, we have to understand something about hip hop.

One of the things that makes hip hop so amazing is that it came from African Americans who had no musical instruments. This is typical of our culture—very much a sign and symbol of what we have always done as African American people. We will produce something out of nothing that will give an explanation, a philosophy, of our resistance.

For example, even though kids growing up in the inner cities of New York and Chicago could not afford musical instruments or take musical lessons, they did have sound, they did have radio, and they did have records. So they decided they would take what they had and make an instrument out of a turntable. That takes a great deal of genius. If we do not have any kinds of musical instruments, we can make instruments out of our bodies or out of our voices. That is where you had guys like the Fat Boys, Bismarkee, and others who became human beat boxes. Whether we want to accept it or not, that takes a lot of genius from today's youth.

The other thing that is interesting about hip hop is that it prides itself on telling the truth. It is a way of giving a message to America that African Americans can take something ordinary and use it for something desirable, or as someone has put it,

> We will take our existence here in the ghetto, even what you perceive as bad: being a gangster, a pimp, or a hustler; and we will tell the story in such a way, in such an art form, that we will make money from it.

Does that not sound similar to the militants who grew up in the sixties? They took a phrase many saw as negative and made it into something positive: "Say it loud. I am black and I am proud." Well, in hip hop that is part of it. Hip hop has changed to the point where it has become a billion-dollar industry.

You have to understand music, to understand and be familiar with some of the major players in hip hop. No longer is it just the political message of Public Enemy or people like KRS One. They are from the old school.

The new school, or hip hop, is influenced by amazing groups like Harmony and people like the Butain Clan or Ghost Space Killer, Method Man, Octagon, and Dirty Old Feet.

People from the Butain Clan tell it like it is. They are real. That is one of the main emphases of today's youth—being real. If profanity is being used in music today, it is largely because they are being real. Butain Clan has become such an industry because they understand marketing. They have developed a whole line of regular street clothing, but they call it "Woo Wear." It will make millions.

Again, you have guys like Ghost Space Killer, Method Man, Roz—and the list goes on and on. Then you have people like James Z; Foxy Brown; and Noz, who has a group called Fern. Foxy Brown and Little Kim would consider themselves the divas of hip hop. If you listen to their music, which is very difficult to do, you will note that they have decided to do what Madonna did. Not to say that that is right, but they, like her, are making money from their sexuality.

So that is why Little Kim and Foxy Brown glamorize the image of being a prostitute. They consider themselves two of the foxes of hip hop. Then you have some of the R&B people like Usher and Genuine, who sing about love and pull the covers off. They do not try to hide anything at all but say exactly what they are doing and what they would do sexually. Do not be too hard on this generation and their music. We need to look at ourselves, too.

People often say that their lyrics are bad—too explicit. But if I can remember when I was coming up in the sixties and seventies, we had some lyrics that were kind of bad, too. For example, "Me and Mrs. Jones—We Got a Thing Going On." Consider another song: "Who's Making Love to Your Old Lady While You're Out Making Love?"

What was any raunchier than the album covers of the Ohio Players? And remember, Skin Right, Fire, and George Clinton did not exactly hide. Someone said Clinton is one of the fathers of hip hop as well. When it comes to our children, especially in the area of music, maybe they were influenced by us.

Movies. A recent survey of 2,018 teens reported in *USA Today* gives insight into the third area of personal interest that is important for us to understand as we know our teens. What is their number one activity? Ninety-one percent of those responding identified going to the movies as their activity of choice. What is significant about this is the taste of the movies they pick. Teens selected R-rated movies as the number one kind of movies they frequent. When it comes to teens going to movies, the question becomes, What kind of movies are they watching?

There is a whole genre of movies targeted to African American youth—movies that have a comical and sometimes sexual theme. One of the movies that has been popular among teens is *Booty Call*, which deals with the antics of two guys who are trying to have sex with two young ladies. The movie deals with one guy's plight as he tries to find a condom before he can have sex.

Another movie that has been out recently is *How to Be a Player*. This movie takes a comical look at how young men can "play" women; in other words, how they can have several different women. Being a player is a main theme among African American men. Again, be careful before you assume this is a new thing because you do remember in the seventies that black exploitation movies really led the way in these things. Maybe the theme was not how to be a player, but we had the theme of how to be a pimp: *Super Fly* and *The Mack*. Our youth may have learned the theme of being a player, a pimp, or a gangster from us. What is going on today with our youth is really nothing new.

Movies today are disturbing because some of them are very violent. It is not just that they are violent, but it is senseless violence—violence where people kill just to be killing. Killing that even has a humorous tone to it. There are so many dead bodies that you become numb to the fact that someone was even shot.

Movies have a strong impact on the way our kids relate, whether it be comedy or even serious love. Even recent movies that target African American youth once again want to keep things real, not necessarily glamorized. Keep it real, and tell it real. Not only are movies important to knowing your child, but the movies often take the place of family. What are our kids doing in their free time?

Couch potatoes. This is a very inactive generation. Our youth would rather listen to their Sony Walkmans or play with their Play Stations or walk in a shopping mall during their free time. For the first time, you have coaches in high school who are having trouble finding enough youth to go out for the football or basketball team, even though many African American youth look at sports as a way of succeeding in adult life.

Image. To your child, image is everything. Madison Avenue realizes this. That is why you cannot pick up a *Source* magazine or a copy of *Vibe*—rap pages targeted to African American youth—without finding that on almost every other page you are going to see references to Tommy Hilfiger jeans, Tanya stereos, or Perry stripes. Again, you will find Triple 5; you will find a variety of clothing articles on almost every page. All of this is targeted to African American teens. Why? Because we are consumers. Image is everything.

Grow with Your Child

Not only is it important to *know* your child, but a missing element when it comes to a parent's connecting with African American youth is *growing* with your child. One of the areas where we have made a mistake is with our quest for authority. Do not misunderstand me. As parents and teachers, we need to establish authority. But one of the balances we need to come back to in relating to our teens is helping them understand that even though I am in authority, I am in a growth process, just like you. As a matter of fact, the Bible makes it clear that *all* of us are in a growth process. That is the language the Bible uses to describe the Christian life. Paul talks about how we are babes in Christ.

The other thing we hear about in Scripture is how we are to mature and grow in Christ. Because we are growing spiritually, our teens need to see that life on every level really is a growth process. One of the things that could help us connect with our youth would be to help our teens see that we are growing with them intellectually, emotionally, and spiritually.

Intellectual growth. If we are expecting teens to grow as students, we need to let them see that we are growing intellectually as well. Learning never stops. When was the last time you discovered something with your teen? When was the last time you began to learn with your teen? This is not to say that we have to be children, but that we need to grow with our children. Give your teen a message that life is one of growing, first of all intellectually.

Emotional growth. Another missing element when it comes to growing with our kids is letting them see that we grow emotionally. Our kids are growing emotionally. Your teens have feelings. Sometimes they do not show it; sometimes we do not provide an atmosphere safe enough for them to show it. Teens have feelings. Unfortunately, some of us grew up in a generation where our parents felt we were too young to have feelings. Our feelings were not validated. Sometimes in the African American community the only feeling we feel comfortable with is the emotion of anger. We have to help our African American youth understand that we have a whole host of feelings. We have feelings that range from fear to anger, from self-confidence to anxiety.

Spiritual growth. Not only do our teens have to see that we are growing intellectually and emotionally, but they have to see that we are growing spiritually as well. As Christian parents, one of the great mistakes we make is not helping our kids see that just as they are on a spiritual journey—trying to live out and grow in what it means to walk with Christ and what it means as far as who they are in Christ—we, too, are growing spiritually. Being the authority in the house does not mean that we have it all together spiritually. That is why family devotions are good, not just because the father and mother, or whoever is in authority, is leading the home spiritually. Being in leadership means that I am growing spiritually, too. We have learned—even in our churches—that pastors have to grow, too. The pastors of the home have to grow as well. It is important for our kids to see we are growing and that we, too, struggle in our prayer life. In addition, we need to spend time in God's Word and model that. Modeling is a key word here. Modeling is assumed when we see parenting as a family affair.

Beyond Rhetoric: Show Your Child

The younger generation does not want more rhetoric.

This is the generation whose highest value is keeping it real. Everything has to be on a *real* trip. This generation is skeptical of our words because they have not seen our models. How do we lead? We lead by example. There are two ways we can lead our children.

First, *how do we handle success?* Do we respond as though success is naturally going to happen, or do we respond with the attitude of Christian parents who understand where success comes from? Do we really teach our kids about success—how to handle success and what it is all about?

Second, *how do we handle failure?* Just as you are responding correctly in showing your child how to respond to success, it is important that we show our children how we deal with failure.

One thing that makes it exciting to be a follower of Christ is the premise of why I need to follow Christ. I accepted what Jesus did on the Cross for my sins because I am indeed a failure. The Bible says, "All have sinned, and come short of the glory of God" (Romans 3:23). The very premise of our Christianity is that we have failed in our efforts to reach God. That is why we have received what Jesus did on the Cross for our sins. So when it comes to the idea of being a failure, will we allow our kids to see us fail? Again, we should be secure. God was so secure in the idea of modeling failure that He publicly allowed His Son to die on the Cross and rise three days later. That is what is exciting about modeling failure to our kids. Not only do we model failure, but we can also model to our kids how they can have victory over their failures, just as we have victory over ours.

When it comes to showing our faith to our kids, the father has to understand that he has a unique role in modeling his life to his son, for the son's self-image will be shaped by the love and affection he receives from his father. It is amazing, but in spite of other influences, it is usually the father who charts the course for his son, because the son's identity is ordinarily established in what he sees in his dad. The son's masculinity will be established by what he sees in his dad. Whether or not his dad affirms that in him, the father plays a unique role in the son's self-image.

The son watches the father on several fronts. He watches how the father loves his mom. From that, he begins to catch a model very early of how a man should relate to and treat a woman. He also sees that from the way the dad interacts with his sister. Once again, even the small things serve as a model. The way he cares for the mom, the way he opens the doors for the mom (oops, that convicts me personally). The way he treats the mom will determine the way this son will express his manhood. Not only is the role of the father important in the son's life (and probably I am saying this because I am a father, and I understand more about this area from a personal level than I do the role for a mother) but also in the life of the daughter.

The role of the father in the life of the daughter is critical because you will be the man she marries. What do I mean by that? When the daughter chooses a husband, many times she will pick a man having many of the same qualities as her dad. The other thing that is frightening is that I have found in my counseling (usually in a public arena when I have spoken on issues like sex) that there is a direct correlation between young ladies who are sexually active and those who do not have a good relationship with their dads. Nine times out of ten, those young ladies will say, "I had a very bad relationship with my father," or "I came from a single-parent home and never had a relationship with my dad."

I am trying not to overgeneralize. Not every young lady who has a bad relationship with her father is involved in a promiscuous relationship. But many times, a poor relationship with a father figure is the case. The father plays a unique role as well in helping the daughter learn to feel like a woman and learn to receive and respond to appropriate affection from the other male figures in her life. Again, daughters long for the attention of a man, and that first longing really is influenced by what they receive from their dad.

Practical Steps

There are some practical steps in the process of knowing,

growing with, and showing our children. The first step is to initiate grace.

An atmosphere of grace. Look at a famous story Jesus told His disciples and the tax collectors, Pharisees, sinners, and scribes standing by when He was illustrating the idea of lostness. Jesus used the illustration of a dysfunctional, or a troubled, family (Luke 15). The story is about two sons. One son decides to get into his rebellious stage and leave home. He does not just leave home, but he asks his father for his inheritance early. That is no small thing. In that culture, you do not receive your inheritance in full until your father dies.

What this son is literally saying is, "Hey, old man. I wish you were dead! Give me my inheritance now."

The father gives the son the inheritance. You know that most African American parents would not have given him his inheritance at all, but simply kicked him out the door. "See ya!" What is interesting is how the father responds. The father gives the son the inheritance, and the son leaves.

The father does not stop the son. He lets him go. He does not lock him away in his room. Luke 15:13–19 says that the son was soon reduced to poverty. He had lost all his money. Read this wonderful story. He comes to his senses and realizes that things are much better at home, even for the hired people. So he decides to go back with a humble attitude, even like one of the servants.

In Luke 15:20, the response of the father is an amazing thing, when you look at it. It speaks to how we should respond to our kids. The Scripture says, "[The son] got up and came to his father. But while he was still a long way off, his father saw him and felt compassion for him, and ran and embraced him and kissed him" (NASB). A couple of things are amazing in that one verse.

One, it says that "while he was still a long way off, his father saw him." That models for us that his dad was *looking* for him, was *expecting* him to come home. When it comes to our kids, we have to expect that—even of the youths we have problems connecting with, even of the kids that seem the most unbearable. The Scripture does not say that while the son was a long way off the dad said, "I am going to sit back and play games. I am not going to make a move toward that delinquent, unappreciative, selfish son of a gun." No. It says while he was a long way off the father ran to the son.

What is amazing about this is that the father had to make some effort to run because the normal attire was a long robe, probably requiring that the father gird it up around himself while he ran. The father went *running* for his son. Not only that, he also kissed him and embraced him. You know what else is interesting? He did all this before the son said a word. What did the father do? He initiated grace.

He did what a counseling friend of mine, Rob Shive, says about stories like this. The father created an atmosphere of grace. He set the environment so the son could return home. When it comes to connecting with our children, the question is, Are we creating an atmosphere of grace? Do our body language and the tone of our voice create an atmosphere where our kids can return home?

Celebration. Not only did the father create an atmosphere of grace—but listen to this—the son said to the father, "I have sinned against heaven and in your sight; I am no longer worthy to be called your son" (Luke 15:21 NASB)

Instead of being vindictive, the father said to his slaves, "Quick! Bring the best robe and put it on him. Put a ring on his finger and sandals on his feet. Bring the fattened calf and kill it. Let's have a feast and celebrate. For this son of mine was dead and is alive again; he was lost and is found" (vv. 22–24 NIV). And they began to be merry. We see nothing about this father's mourning his son's leaving, but we do see him celebrating his return.

I like that. When I look at this story it says that when the son comes back the father celebrates. It does not say he said, "You should not have left in the first place. I am glad you came to your senses. I am tired of your being so trifling. You are going to be thankful one day that you had a father like me." We see nothing in this man's attitude like that. He celebrates his son's return.

Boundaries. The father did something else that is another practical step for us. He set appropriate boundaries. Boundaries are a defined property line. The father gave the son what he asked for. Another interesting thing is that the father did not allow the son to cause problems in his house. He did not close the business to look for the son. He did not go after him.

He respected the son's boundaries. He gave the son his rightful inheritance even though the son was not yet entitled to it. He also allowed the son to experience the whirlwind predicted in Galatians 6:7: "God is not mocked: for whatsoever a man soweth, that shall he also reap."

The father allowed the son to reap the repercussions of his choices. Often when it comes to our youth today, we do not allow that. This area really does take the wisdom of the Holy Spirit to lead and guide you, but often we protect our youth to the point where they do not understand what the consequences are to their choices. That father allowed his son to reap those consequences. He allowed the son to learn valuable lessons through his pain.

Compassion. Another practical step in the process of this family affair is that the father had compassion for his child. Verse 20 says he sympathized with him. Sometimes we forget that the things our teens are going through are very painful. Sometimes we forget that there are a lot of difficult things going on today our teens have to deal with. Some teens in some areas of the country may be just trying to survive the day without getting shot or beat up. Often we forget how difficult adolescence is. We do not sympathize with our children.

I like what Romans 12 says: "Rejoice with those who rejoice; mourn with those who mourn" (v. 15 NIV). And boy! Do you need to begin to do that with your kids!

A game plan. Develop a game plan when it comes to connecting with your child. Spend thirty minutes of uninterrupted one-to-one time with your child once a week. That sounds like it is too little, but some of us have not been spending any time at all. Hopefully you will move to thirty minutes a day; but if you are not spending any time at all, start small and be committed to that time. During that time you should apologize when that is appropriate. If you are wrong, say you are wrong. Also, find out how your child feels about home, and do not be defensive. Find out how he or she feels about you. Decide that you will listen more than talk. Tell your child how you feel, but preface it with, "You know, I might not see things correctly. I might be wrong."

Inventory. Set goals for your family. Meet with your youth pastor or youth worker to talk about what you can do as a parent. Then take an inventory of your relationships. *Do I create an atmosphere of compassion in my home? Can my youth approach me?* Invite another parent to evaluate how you are doing as a parent because—let me tell you something—you are not alone. When it comes to connecting with our youth today, it really is a family affair. It will go beyond what the youth worker can do, but it is going to take three things.

First, *know your child.* Know who your child is, and understand what your child is listening to. Understand the atmosphere your child lives in. Understand your child's music. Even listen to some of your child's music! I am not saying you need a regular diet of it. I am not saying you need to go out and purchase Mace and Pup Daddy and the Wootan Clan. I am not saying that at all. But I am saying, know your child. Go to the movies with him or her. If a film violates your standards as a Christian family, calmly explain why and select another one that is acceptable.

Second, *grow with your child.* The longer I am a believer, the more I am thankful that God realizes that I am growing. What is important is that this generation needs to see that we are growing as well. We can grow together.

Finally, *show your child.* That takes the power of the Holy Spirit. Lead by example. Your actions will speak louder than your words. This generation has heroes they feel are heroes because of what they *showed.*

Michael Jordan shows us on the basketball court. Tiger Woods does not just talk golf; he shows us what it means to be a golfer. Why do we like Alan Iverson? He shows us. Other aspects of his life may be out of whack, but at least he can show us basketball. Why do I like Jesus? Because He shows us through His death on the Cross and His resurrection that He is *for* us. How can we connect with our kids? We have to show them as well.

Finally, when it comes to connecting with our youth, we are all in the same boat. It really is a family affair, not just in your home, but also when it comes to who we are in the body of Christ. To quote the African proverb, "It takes a village to raise a child."

James White (Cary, N.C.) is a speaker for Campus Crusade for Christ.

Chapter 6

Beyond Programs

BY ROBIN S. DICKSON AND ROBERTA KITCHEN

When I think of the youth meetings at our church, my mind goes immediately to Easter and Christmas pageants, car washes, candy sales, pizza and pop lock-ins, preparing for pastor's appreciation, the church's anniversary, the junior deacons, junior ushers, and junior nurses—just to name a few. To be sure, there was always plenty of "stuff" to do.

Speaking of "stuff," who could forget the infamous Youth Day that came faithfully, once each year, generally on the fifth Sunday of a month? Such was a time of frenzied excitement because the youth were to "take charge of the services." A special "choir" was formed, composed of any youth wanting to participate. Colors and dress code were established, and a theme for the program was passed down from the pastor and/or youth directors.

Selections were then made for such speaking parts as the

mistress/master of ceremonies, the welcome, and history of the department. The Sunday school or Junior Deacons led the devotional period.

Included in the program, generally, was a poem or thought on the theme—recited or read by a very nervous young person, as proud loved ones supported him (or her) with loud amens and applause. The pastor then introduced the speaker (sometimes he was relevant). After all the whooping and shouting ended, a delicious dinner would be served on the grounds. It would be touted as the best Youth Day ever.

Makes you wonder with so much "stuff" going on why so few of us as young people actually came to a saving knowledge of God and His plan for our lives.

We grew up in the church and felt we were part of the church. Whether we went because our parents made us (remember when you couldn't go to the movies if you didn't go to church?), or because we wanted to be with our friends—going to church was the thing to do back then.

As we grew older, however, we found that our kinship with the church had little to do with our kinship to Jesus Christ. We had been so busy with the "stuff" the church offered us as youth that we really had not established a relationship with the Person in whose name we came to worship or, more accurately, the One whose program the church was carrying out. For many of us, Sunday morning was not a time of worship, but a meeting time, where we came together in a time-honored tradition filled with many rituals, including the "stuff" that comprised the youth ministry. Few felt God really cared—rather that He sat somewhere watching, waiting to pounce on us the minute we slipped. And slip we did.

A New Day

Today much has changed. There is a genuine movement on the part of African American youth to find meaning and purpose in their lives. As they are seeking answers, they are simultaneously being sought by a myriad of callers. Each day our youth are bombarded by the siren calls of pop culture calling them to destruction, just as the sirens of ancient Roman and Greek legends called sailors to their destruction with their sweet singing. Gangs call our youth; drugs call our youth; youth call other youth to join them in vice and crime; fame and fortune call; dreams call.

What do these callers possess that makes their voices so compelling? In a time when there so much dysfunctionality and brokenness, they offer what young people crave—a sense of belonging, security, unconditional love, trust, respect, discipline, boundaries, and consequences.

What exactly do our youth need, and what role does the church play in meeting that need? Though they might articulate their needs differently, what we believe they need is parenting! A healthy emphasis on empowering parents will allow the church to rise up with answers that touch the needs of young people. We believe it is about three words: *challenge, commitment,* and *hope.*

In this age of so much dysfunctionality, the African American church must wise up. What we used to do will not work today. We must challenge our high school and college youth to come near to a God who wants a relationship and communion with them. We must make a commitment to them to nurture them in that relationship, and we must make the hope that we have in God real in their lives.

The dictionary defines *parent* as "one that begets or brings forth . . . offspring; a person who brings up and cares for another; . . . a group from which another arises and to which it usu. remains subsidiary" (*Merriam-Webster's Collegiate Dictionary*, 1997).

Parenting high school and college youth is all about building relationships of trust and respect so that our youth are inspired to follow our example. The church so often admonishes the young person on what to do but fails to show him or her how to do it. For example, the counsel to call on God when you need Him is good, but how do you go to someone you can't see; and how can you tell when you have gotten there? Our youth know most times *what* to do; they just don't know how.

Just as the doting parent in getting a toddler to walk first stands him on shaky little legs and then patiently coaxes him to move toward themselves, so the church must place its youth in a position where they will come to know the God who created them.

Though that toddler has never walked alone before, he trusts his father or mother enough to lift one tiny little foot and advance toward them. Though justifiably elated over this accomplishment, that parent must not be satisfied that the toddler makes his first tiny step, but must continue to coax and encourage him until he is able to walk alone. Individual steps are not walking.

So the church cannot be satisfied with Sunday morning, Wednesday night, or youth night church attendance alone. It must encourage and challenge youth to move beyond the initial steps of church attendance to truly walking and communing with God in the spirit.

Our youth are growing up in a world much different from the one in which we grew up. So the challenge to the African American church is greater than ever before, not simply to parent the youth within our midst, but to reach out to the youth who otherwise may never cross the threshold of the church. The traditional ministries of our churches do not apply because those ministries are designed to parent offspring, children, and young adults who are born and raised in our churches, to whom God is at least known and to whom God will become real.

But what about those young people who do not know God, who have no recollection of being sent to Sunday school or church, even on Easter, Christmas, and Mother's Day? No recollection of praying parents and grandparents. No frame of reference that includes God and His Son, Jesus Christ, our Lord and Savior. These are the children in our neighborhoods and in our schools for whom we are indeed the only Jesus they will see. These are the youth we must reach out to parent, for they will not come to us.

Just as Christ came to seek and save the lost, so the African American church must reach out to youth who are unchurched, who have no parenting church, and all too often who have no parenting parents.

"For I know the plans I have for you," declares the Lord, "plans to prosper you and not to harm you, plans to give you hope and a future." (Jeremiah 29:11 NIV)

Ask God for His plans concerning your youth. Then plan your meetings accordingly, understanding that your plans for the group's direction might not necessarily be His plans.

During a staff meeting, God spoke to us directly from passages in Exodus 28–30 concerning His plans for our youth group:

> And take thou unto thee Aaron thy brother, and his sons with him, from among the children of Israel, that he may minister unto me in the priest's office, even Aaron, Nadab and Abihu, Eleazar and Ithamar, Aaron's sons. (Exodus 28:1)

As we studied and meditated over these passages, we initially felt that God was instructing us concerning our role as priests before the young people with whom we worked. However, as the evening wore on and in the days that followed, it became increasingly clear to us that God was likening us to the role of Moses in these passages, and that we were to prepare the young people for ministry (Exodus 28:3; 28:41; 29:9, 33–35; 30:30). It *did* make sense, after all, as we realized that many of the young people in our small group did not attend church—neither did many of their friends at school or their relatives, for that matter. God's plan would involve using these young people to expand the ministry He had given to us!

In light of this revelation, we changed the emphasis of our weekly meetings. Pulling information from any sources we could find, we began intense Bible study on such topics as knowing God, Christ and the Holy Spirit, prayer and fasting, Satan and deception, end times, spiritual warfare, intercession, relationships, racism, pain and abuse (physical, mental), and leadership. We began cultivating a "sense of other" in our youth every opportunity we got. We took them across town or out of town to be among people who did not look like them.

In each instance, we found practical ways to bring God's truth home.

For instance, in our lessons on knowing the Godhead, we concentrated on the significance of names in biblical times. We presented them with research we'd done on the meanings of their names and shared in part some of what God was revealing to us concerning His plans for their lives. The transformation that took place in them as they, for the first time, glimpsed God's call on them was phenomenal. For them, God had come near.

We went further, by challenging them to take personal inventory of the names they so innocently ascribed to in their dress, music, videos, recreation, and walk. We asked them to write people like Tommy Hilfiger, Nike executives, and others whose name they have chosen to represent. Specifically, they were to inquire of that individual's walk with God while sharing how important they believed it was for these individuals to come to a saving knowledge of Christ. This was a tall order. Needless to say, our youth weren't overly excited about the project. But we have challenged them to walk worthy of the profession to which they have been called. To be sure, our little group of teens looks more like a band of outlaws than priests—but so did Aaron's team.

We challenged other youth leaders to pray for "spirit eyes" that they might see the gifting God has placed in their young people and begin to train them in the "way that they should go."

Knowing God Personally

This is eternal life, that they may know You, the only true God, and Jesus Christ whom You have sent. (John 17:3 NASB)

Moses went up in the mountains to meet Him; Job cried out in the night for Him; Paul's desire was to know God. These men sought God because they desired something more from Him than merely knowing He was there for them.

Directed quiet time. Recently our 24-Seven Christian Ministry took a group of teens on a retreat held in an area abundant with trees and trails. Our theme for that weekend was "R U 4 Real?" We assembled about fifteen youth early one morning to meet with God alone.

These young people, ranging from twelve to nineteen years of age, believed that God existed. If asked, they would even tell you that God existed for them. But apart from knowing some superficial facts about God, few, if any, knew God in a personal way. So on this particular morning, we sent them out laden with Bible, journal, pen, and the following instructions:

> During the next forty-five minutes, find a spot where you can be alone with God. Spend the time walking and talking with God; or find a solitary place to sit. Talk to no one other than God. Ask or tell Him anything. Talk out loud to Him. No one will be near enough to hear you but God. Focus your thoughts on Him. Tell Him how you feel about Him. Ask Him to speak with you. Record your experience in your journal by answering the questions on page six.

What follows is a sample of their reactions to this exercise. Note particularly the responses to the last question, "What happened during this time that was especially meaningful or joyful?"

How did you feel as you walked and talked with God?

"I felt safe and nervous at the same time."

"I was getting all of my feelings out about the way I felt about things in my life. I felt sad, and happy. I had a lot of different feelings."

"With me being by (myself) I felt comfortable to know I could talk to Him."

"I felt nervous and unsure, didn't know what to say, very ignorant."

"Pretty good. Thankful, mostly."

"It felt good and peaceful to talk to God."

"To me it felt as if no one was listening to what I said, but I know God was listening to what I said."

What part of your love relationship with God did you become most aware of?
"How we need to have a better relationship than we do. And talk to Him more."
"I became aware that I can have a better relationship with Him."
"That God is a forgiving God."
"The part of a love relationship that I was most aware of is different than most people because I talk to God sort of through nature, like the sky and water. And when I talk to Him I feel that I'm free and that I can say anything and He will understand."
"His mercifulness, forgiveness, blessings."
"That my relationship is not strong with God and can become stronger."

Was this difficult or an emotionally uneasy time for you? Why do you think it was?
"It was not difficult for me because I told Him how I feel, and He would not feel any less of me, and He will help me."
"I was telling God that I wish all the sadness and pain would stop happening in my life."
"More so emotional, because I know God was looking down on me."
"The time I spend talking to God or talking about religion is the difficult time for me, because I don't know what to say."
"Yes, it was difficult, but I don't exactly know why."

What happened during this time that was especially meaningful or joyful?
"That I really took time out to talk to Him and told Him how I really feel."
"The most meaningful and joyful part was I really, for the first time, took the time to talk to God and tell Him how I feel and really opened my heart to Him."
"I felt that God began to love me a bit more and my do-

ings."
"I feel my inner self and my inner strength, and I feel that no one can bring me down except God."
"Nothing."
"Going to the school, graduation, to go to college and major in business."
"That I had a chance to talk to God for a few minutes."

I don't think our teens will soon forget this experience. We cannot overemphasize the importance of placing your teens in a position where they can meet and talk to God one-to-one. We are not saying that this is the only way a youth comes to know God personally, but for sure it works.

Small groups. Break up those big youth groups into small groups. Challenge your youth to get to know God by searching for Him in His Word. The Scripture says, "The word of God is . . . sharper than any two-edged sword, and piercing as far as the division of soul and spirit" (Hebrews 4:12 NASB). Plan lessons that address needs youth are presently experiencing. Show clearly in the Scripture how God is present in their personal situations.

Don't wait for youth to decide to come to your meetings. God did not wait for you to come to Him: He sought you through His Spirit (Matthew 18:11). Provide transportation for youth to attend your meetings. Schedule meetings in the neighborhood recreation center in order to include those youth who may not be eager to enter a church.

Lead them past the basketball court and game rooms to a quiet place to talk seriously about kingdom business. Recreation certainly has its place; but too many times the Gospel presentation is made on the tail end of a night of fun and games as though our youth were not capable of committing to a relationship based solely upon the presentation of the Gospel.

For too many years we have been deceived into thinking that we must soft-pedal the Gospel because youth are unwilling to receive such strict disciplines. We have found the opposite to be true. Young people face hard temptations, tough situations, and big decisions every day. They need a store-house of knowledge and a means to research God's Word on their own to deal with the difficult times in their lives.

"Just Say No!" is not enough. They need to know *why* God wants them to say no before they are asked to say yes. Not only will they be grateful to you for sharing God's plan for their lives, but they will share God's plan with their peers. They will happily report their attempts and their successes in your weekly youth meetings.

Journaling. Several years ago we began creating journals for our trips. The journals are simple and generally require the youth to answer specific questions designed to help them critique their experiences while on the trip. These journals are valuable tools in helping us assess where our youth are spiritually.

Young people attending college need support, especially if they are away from home where they may become bombarded with non-Christian religions, godless philosophies, and other subtle teachings that threaten to weaken and destroy their faith if they are not exposed to countervailing influences.

As a church body, set aside special nights for letter writing, preparing care packages, and holding special prayer meetings where each youth's name is lifted before the Lord and specific requests are made for each young person.

Remember, the enemy is looking for any crack in their armor as an opportunity to wear them down and draw them away from the faith to which they are committed. Offer special services for rededication and recommitment for your college youth prior to their returning to college after each school break.

Locate friends and other church families in the localities where your teens will be living, and have them commit to becoming foster parents. Assign members/teams of other youth to keep communications open between college life and home through letters, phone calls, visits, and holding one another accountable.

Include the computer in your communications arsenal!

Use E-mail to keep in touch with your college students. Design a home page for your church, and encourage your young people to contribute to the content. Web sites offer unlimited potential for youth ministry—keeping in touch and reaching out to surfers on the net.

Laying on of hands. Prayer—before, during, and after all activities—is as essential to youth ministry as it is to all undertakings we attempt for God. Pray for guidance, for protection, for your efforts to bear fruit. Pray for the young people you serve and their families. Enlist prayer from the youth themselves. Enlist the prayers of your church family and other supporters.

We have made a point of taking pictures of all our youth members and later, during our staff meetings, placing our hands on each image and praying specifically for that youth's life and God's plans therefor. God honors the "effectual fervent prayer of a righteous man" (James 5:16).

Meet Lee, a fifteen-year-old African American who was struggling with drugs. Lee had been a member of our group for several years. Though he did not attend every meeting, you could always count on his presence adding a new dimension to the meetings he did attend. Frequent drug and alcohol use had taken a physical toll on Lee. This tall, lanky, chocolate-skinned boy of a man was not what you'd like to have come calling on your daughter. In fact, if you didn't know Lee, you wouldn't have liked him very much at all. He lived with a grandmother and a house full of uncles and others. The young people often complained when he'd show up at the van for a ride to the meeting drunk or high, but you could count on his bringing along some of his buddies. Sometimes Lee slept at the meetings. Other times he actively participated in the discussion. On the surface, Lee would have been considered a loser—except for his name—God called him to be a priest!

I suppose if there is one critical thing we have learned in our experience working with youth it is this: *Never, ever take for granted what the Holy Spirit is doing in your meetings, and never ever close out a meeting without providing your youth the opportunity to accept Christ.* During one meeting, after a lively discussion on how Satan—like God—planned for our future, Lee joined with several others in praying to receive Jesus. There were no emotional outbursts or tears but a simple time of bowing our heads and praying for forgiveness. Lee had a lot of questions about salvation and about his relatives who were involved in Islam. I would remember those moments some three years later.

It was September 27, 1996, at one o'clock in the afternoon. It was raining outside. We were at church, and it was crammed full of young people. They came in limos, big cars, small cars, bikes. But a steady stream of them, nevertheless, filed in to see one called to be a priest. In their hands were copies of an obituary of a young man who had died of a drug overdose five days earlier. This would be Lee's last youth meeting on this side of eternity. But true to his calling, Lee brought more of his peers together in his dying than most of us do in our lifetime. Some heard the Gospel for the very first time.

We don't know what work was going on in the hearts of these young people, but many a face registered shock when they found out Lee was in heaven with God. They had never heard that salvation is by grace alone. We held them as they wept over the absence of their friend. We may never know what the Holy Spirit was doing in those young hearts, but we do know God's Word does not return to Him void.

Robin S. Dickson is director of 24-Seven Christian Club (Euclid, Ohio). *Roberta Kitchen* is director of 24-Seven Christian Club (Cleveland, Ohio).

Chapter 7

Running the Relay Race with Our Youth

**BY REV. GERALD AUSTIN, SR., AND
WILLIAM C. SINGLETON III**

Every day we witness parents coming together to reclaim their neighborhoods. We see students helping each other in our weekly youth meetings, tutoring sessions, job initiatives, business development program, and summer camp. We have watched black and white volunteers and staff work together with a single purpose—bringing permanent change to our community, which is full of promise and need.

Five Unifying Principles

Five fundamental principles must be embraced if permanent change is to occur in parenting our high school and college youth. If the public and private sectors take these principles to heart, the future of our youth will improve to the praise and glory of God's grace.

Principle 1: All are created in the image of God.
When I met Mrs. Ora Stinson eleven years ago, she had two

boys, seven and ten years of age. She was functionally illiterate, living in Birmingham, Alabama, in a downtown community called Metropolitan Gardens, zip code 35203, cited as the poorest zip code in the nation.

Through the programs of the Center for Urban Missions (hereinafter, the Center), Mrs. Stinson not only learned to read, but soon became the president of the parent-teacher association at her son's elementary school. Mrs. Stinson is presently working as a full-time secretary/receptionist for the Center. She drives a Pentium-based computer, fully loaded with word processor and spreadsheet, and handles her job with much expertise. Mrs. Stinson's son Martin, now twenty-one, has completed two years of college and is presently working as a bench technician in our low-tech manufacturing plant, making a living wage. Her other son, Seneca, is a senior in high school and will be graduating this May.

Each person, irrespective of his or her background, has unique God-given potential. Through God's intervention, each person can become everything he or she was created to be, for we are created in the image of God. As we work with high school and college youth, this basic presupposition provides the hope and optimism to hang in there when the going gets tough. It helps our youth overcome the difficulties they face because they are relying on a hope greater than their obstacles. This reality also enables those who are disciplers in the community of need to have the hope they need to hang in there and support our young people through some of the difficulties they experience in their lives.

From the standpoint of policy, this means that any strategy to parent our high school and college youth which omits an emphasis on spiritual values is misplaced. As a nation, we must move toward greater accommodation of religious values. In the public sector, the Supreme Court must continue to move toward a less restricted view of the first amendment. Federal, state, and local governments must be free to give neutral benefits to religious groups to the extent that they address the problems besetting our families. In the private sector, corporations and foundations should look to form partnerships with these groups as well. We must form these vital relationships to empower our youths to achieve their goals.

Principle 2: We are our brother's keeper. The next step in addressing the critical issue of parenting our high school and college youth is to recognize that we are under a moral obligation to do so. We have to recognize that the problems in urban America are not black problems or white problems, but *our* problems. We have to understand that a city or household divided against itself will not stand.

From a policy perspective, we must encourage and make it possible for governments, businesses, churches, and strategic organizations to work together to assume their duties to address our shared communities' needs. From an individual perspective, we must encourage one another to assume responsibility to address the problems of our neighbors, irrespective of who they are.

In 1989, I met William C. Singleton III, a metro reporter for the *Birmingham Post-Herald* while he was doing an article on the Center. After the interview, William couldn't help but wonder how we got people from different denominations, various socioeconomic groups, and multiple racial backgrounds, in both the public and the private sector, to come together to work with our young people in the city. William's intrigue led him to visit one of the Center's Friday Night Bible Club programs. William was impressed with the program, but he noticed that there weren't many African American men participating. Soon after, Bill became a volunteer, more out of responsibility than experience.

William's background is very different from mine. He came from a two-parent family, grew up in suburban Maryland, in Prince Georges County—the county with the richest concentration of black wealth in the nation. A single-parent family in William's neighborhood was the exception rather than the rule. William conveyed to me that his father was always there for him. However, I grew up in a single-parent family, one of nine children, raised by my loving mother. All nine of us were able to go to college and establish careers.

While working for General Electric Medical Systems division as a field engineer, I felt the call of God to full-time ministry. The ministry to which I was called was the community from which I had emerged. Growing up, I had learned from many father figures. There were the "Uncle Docs" and "Brother Kings" in my life. From these positive adult males, I drew strength. They were the kind of role models not often found today in our urban communities. Doc Motley was an older gentleman who would take us down to church with him on Saturdays to clean up. And he would take us with him as he ran errands on Saturdays.

Brother King, an elderly church member at Mount Zion Community Church, played a role in nurturing my siblings and me as he discussed life issues with us. I remember sitting as a wide-eyed young man listening to great stories of how Doc was able to provide for his wife and children by working hard.

There were also people like Louis Humphreys—white Christians who helped disciple me in the early years of my Christian experience. Today, there are brothers like Roy Gilbert, Charlie Webb, and Drayton Nabors—prominent businessmen and mentors who have encouraged me throughout my ministry.

In 1990, the Lord led my wife and me to start The New City Church. We began with nine African American families and three white families. Our church has grown from those twelve families to over 150 families who are actively involved in our church. Our church provides a wonderful continuum for discipling our youth (from the street to the sanctuary). Because our church is located in the very heart of the city, it provides easy access to and an opportunity to be a visible witness in the historic center city area where many families live. We have a growing men's discipleship group, and the men in our church are assuming increasing responsibility to provide the necessary modeling and covering for our youth.

Through the Center's programs we provide a variety of educational initiatives, such as tutoring programs and Bible clubs, to help students achieve academically and spiritually.

These programs provide excellent opportunities for volunteers to demonstrate the fact that we are our brother's keeper. Through the programs, relationships are forged with the youth. These young people interact with positive role models, something they need to offset the image of drug pushers, dropouts, and gang members who occupy permanent spots on the street corners of their communities.

In many ways, volunteers, especially African American men, become surrogate parents for the youth. This fact is evidenced in the way the youth relate to such adults as William Singleton, Brent Mitten, Tracy Hipps, Dereck Jackson, and Archie Johnson. These men have become a major influence in the lives of our young people. In a day when traditional family units are becoming a rarity, we need to heed the African proverb "It takes a village to raise a child." Our villages must discover the need to serve one another because it is right. "We are our brother's keeper" is an important philosophy that provides a framework for our commitment to parenting our urban youth.

Principle 3: Begin with the family in mind. To effectively address the critical problem of parenting youth, attention must be focused on the entire family system rather than on individuals alone. Many of our efforts have been counterproductive because they were designed to meet the needs of the individual without understanding the larger context in which the needs arose. At the Center and New City Church, we see ourselves as part of a global community made up of family systems as opposed to discrete individuals. The idea of radical individualism is a Western concept. Most of the world identifies itself in a more relational way.

We constantly seek to join forces with the whole person, the whole family, and the whole community when we find a family in need. Families are the basic building block of any society; and if we are to effectively address the problems of individuals, we must look at the family strategically. Families are multifaceted institutions and therefore require a multifaceted strategy with a single focus. In our individual and corporate efforts, we must work to eliminate the current hodgepodge of individualistic services directed toward serving families. In addressing the whole family and the whole person, we develop synergy that produces permanent change.

Principle 4: Base actions on empowerment. If we really believe that our young people can overcome the problems and obstacles they face, we should direct our efforts toward empowering them to do so rather than simply providing relief. The person who earns his way controls his destiny. I often communicate to our constituency that we have no giveaways. Even the salvation we enjoy cost God His Son Jesus. The person who only receives is owned by the giver. Thus, giveaways should be avoided unless absolutely necessary. It is vital to the self-esteem of those whom we are serving, our young people, that we act and behave responsibly in our efforts to help improve their plight. We must not patronize our young people with *handouts*, but rather inspire them with a *hand up*.

Education and skill development are essential to the empowerment of those we seek to serve. To receive any benefit in our programs, work is required. We are seeing the fruit of our labors as families acquire the tools they need to overcome the hurdles they face. As a matter of policy, helpers should dramatically reduce the programs that merely provide relief and insist on incentive-based initiative. The former rob recipients of dignity; the latter can help them regain the self-confidence needed to compete in an increasingly challenging national economy.

Principle 5: Who you are is more important than what you say. A study sponsored by the Robert Woods Johnson Foundation reviewed the effectiveness of anti-drug and safe-sex messages given by many of our national leaders, such as the "Say no to drugs" and "Just do it" campaigns. The study found the messages were ineffective and concluded that there is no effective way to reach urban youth on these subjects.

The study's conclusion was wrong. There *is* an effective way to reach urban youth. What is required is a messenger whom they know and trust. We must be messengers willing to live out what we say—messengers who have an innate drive to care, a passion to serve, and a desire to see our youth empowered.

Previously I mentioned people such as William Singleton III, Brent Mitten, Archie Johnson, Dereck Jackson, and Tracy Hipps. This is not just a list of names. Embedded in their collective history with the Center and New City Church are the five unifying principles that will increase our success in parenting our youth.

Making the Baton Exchange

The metaphor of passing the baton is an appropriate one. Every sprinter or long distance runner who has ever powered a leg on a relay team understands the crucial, yet delicate, art of the baton exchange. No matter how fast the first runner gets out of the starting blocks or the second runner makes up the stagger on the curve, if one of the team members drops the baton, the race is virtually lost.

William Singleton recalls an incident from his high school track days that illustrates this point. His high school 800-meter relay team was one of the best in the state. But days before the regional track meet that would decide which teams would advance to the finals, their best sprinter got kicked off the track team. The person who took his place was Tracy, their long jumper who occasionally ran relays with the practice team. The team was disappointed that their best runner would not be competing, but they believed they could still win and qualify for the state tournament.

On the day of the race, the first runner, Stacey, took a comfortable lead. As he prepared to hand off, Tracy started moving before Stacey reached him. Stacey extended his arm forward to pass the baton but met only air and tumbled to the ground, the baton spinning on the rubber track surface. Tracy stopped and stared in bewilderment at the baton and his fallen teammate, wondering what he should do. After hearing the crowd, several teammates, and their track coach shout, "Pick it up! Pick it up!" Tracy grabbed the baton, but the damage had already been done. Even though the team made a valiant effort to make up ground, the errant baton exchange cost them a place in the state tournament.

William and his teammates were disappointed because they had wasted a great opportunity. But the spiritual insight from the incident would prove to be better than any imitation gold medal they would have received for winning the state championship.

When we talk about parenting high school youth, especially African American males who have no father figures in the home, we are speaking in track terms. We are talking about running a relay race with the children of the inner city as the baton. That image may seem impersonal. It is not, however, when you realize the care and delicacy it takes to handle a baton and execute the successful exchange crucial in a team's efforts to win a relay race. Runners who are not on the same page and not operating with a single purpose risk dropping the baton. That is devastating when we consider that the baton represents youths we are trying to rescue. Even the apostle Paul considered the sport of track a fitting metaphor when he urged believers in Christ to "run the race" and to have the mentality of a marathon runner in their Christian faith (1 Corinthians 9:24).

At the Center, we have taken this concept to heart. We are blessed with volunteers like William Singleton, full-time staff members Brent Mitten and Dereck Jackson, Tracy Hipps (youth director for the Center and youth pastor of New City Church), and Archie Johnson (professional athlete and youth worker). The precious lives of our young people are being impacted positively by men who serve as role models in the various stages of their lives.

William Singleton III recalls his experience as part of our "relay race" in the remainder of this chapter.

I (William) remember when I first started to volunteer at the Center in 1989. The children's Bible study program was being run out of a community recreation center where many of the youths congregated to play pool and other games. I was assigned four youths, ages nine to eleven. One of those young men was Antonio Hill, whom friends and family call "Muggy."

Muggy was a rotund little tyke, almost introverted if not for his Spanky-like playfulness. (Spanky was the pudgy leader of the Little Rascals.)

Muggy lacked the leadership personality of a Spanky, however, or at least that is what I thought initially. Muggy wasn't the ringleader of any of the clusters of young boys who would filter through the recreation center—just the opposite of his cousin, Patrick, whose intelligence and charm radiated through even a streetwise demeanor.

But one quality Muggy possessed was perseverance. He would come to Friday night Bible study faithfully, even though it was sometimes hard to tell if anything was sinking in. To reward the students for coming to Bible study, I would take them roller skating or to the mall, invite them to picnics sponsored by my employer, and take them other places. It was during those outings that I shared with them about life, opening up to them my personal life, my dating relationships, and other heartfelt things young people were interested in between those Bible study times.

I remember Muggy and the other guys asking me whether I had any children. When I responded, "No," the look on their faces seemed to suggest that such a concept was foreign to them, particularly since at the time I was a single man and free to be a "Mack Daddy," as they saw it. But Muggy enjoyed being able to escape his public housing environment, and his mother was grateful that someone had taken an interest in her son.

My relationship with Muggy continued until Brent Mitten took over in 1991. Brent is a white brother from Canada who answered God's call to come to Birmingham by straddling his Honda CB 750-Custom motorcycle and riding the three thousand miles it took to get here. He believed God called him to work with inner-city youth. Initially, Mitten had reservations about how to build a relationship with the young boys who were different from him, not only by skin color but also by culture.

"I was concerned about the differences: the difference in coming from another country, the differences in cultures,"

Mitten says. "But that was made easier because of the relationship and trust that had already been established with Muggy, Jermaine, Pat, and Marcus."

Mitten asked me one day if I would be offended if he started to build a relationship with the guys with whom I had been working since they were among the more faithful guys from the neighborhood attending Center programs. I reassured Mitten that we were a part of the same mission and that he actually could do more with the young boys and develop a closer relationship with them since he was going to be working with them on almost a full-time basis. It didn't take Mitten long to develop a relationship with Muggy and the other guys, allowing me to begin pursuing relationships with some of the other young kids.

Following the track analogy, Mitten became the second member of the relay team and built upon the lead that had been established. Mitten involved Muggy and the other youths in ministry-oriented outreaches, such as the summer camp ministry, which combines teaching of the Word, recreational activities, and academics. Mitten also instructed many of the young people from Metropolitan Gardens during Wednesday night Bible study at New City Church.

Mitten then passed the baton to Dereck Jackson, who came to the Center in 1993 and coordinates the Living Proof ministry training team. Living Proof, as Jackson explains it, is a team of youths who are learning to reach their peers for Christ and become more involved in understanding their roles as leaders of the ministry that birthed and nurtured them. "I saw the vision that I had of what ministry ought to be, which is coming alongside people and developing relationships, encouraging people, and challenging people in their daily walk with Christ," Jackson says. "That was something I didn't have when I was coming up in high school."

Muggy, now eighteen, is one of the members of the leadership team. "It's a big step for me because they're teaching me how to do evangelism and bring my peers to Christ. It's scary a little bit because I don't know how people are going to react. I don't like to get rejected, but I do want to help my peers," says Muggy, still circular, with an offensive lineman's body and a crucifix dangling from a chain about his neck. Muggy acknowledges that he has come a long way from days when he would tag along to Metro Experience simply because of his friends. Muggy remains connected to the Center and New City Church.

"At first I wasn't really into God. I didn't know much about Him, and I wasn't really listening to the lesson. But now that I've gotten older, I realize I have to take it personally," he says. "I realize I can't be foolish all the time because God is nobody to play with."

There have been setbacks in Muggy's development. He was dismissed from school because of a general lack of interest in his studies and a playful attitude. "He has realized the seriousness of that and has made efforts to get his GED and a technical skill," Mitten says. "His consistency in coming to the church and recognizing some spiritual growth is a testimony to the fact that he wants to do right. I think he wants to serve the Lord. It has really been fun to watch him discover himself—his own identity apart from the group he used to always hang out with."

Muggy was attending a local junior college in Birmingham to get his GED but had to put that on hold. He plans to return to the college to complete his GED. He later wants to attend a Christian college, where he will pursue studies in the field of ministry training. For a youth who has very little contact with his real father, Muggy says men like Mitten and Jackson have filled that gap in his life. "All of y' all are like fathers to me because y' all have always been there," Muggy says.

Muggy is not the only success story. There's Lakisha Godfrey, a cherub-cheeked ninth grader who became involved with the Center and New City Church when she was in the third grade. Kisha, as she likes to be called, got involved in the Center's Scholar's Club program and received a scholarship to attend school at Briarwood Presbyterian Church, an upscale Christian school in a high income community on the outskirts of Birmingham.

Becca, another worker, recalls, "When I met Kisha, she

was trying to survive in a suburban white school. I was the white driver on whom she took out her daily anguishes. It is no secret that Kisha and I had trouble finding a middle ground the first year we associated with each other. By the end of the eighth grade, however, we both noticed a change. Kisha had become a much softer, more controlled young woman. We laughed about the past and formed a friendship. Today Kisha meets regularly with a group of high school girls and me. Her love of God and desire to continue in her walk with Him is evident in a lot of what she does. Controlling her anger was something Kisha always had trouble with. Today, I've not only seen her control it, but I've seen that the minute, 'worldly' things that used to bother her, don't affect her anymore. Kisha has begun ministering to her peers. Immediately, she became a key player in Living Proof, our youth group. Still only a freshman, Kisha is doing great things."

There is also Eddie Casey who could put a special prosecutor to shame with his multiple questions about life. "When I first met Eddie, he drove me nuts. He just asked all kinds of questions," Mitten says. "But once I started to get to know Eddie, I realized he was just a curious little boy." As Mitten teaches Eddie about the things of God, that natural curiosity comes forth. "We were at a football game at the kickoff, and the guy was about to catch the ball. Eddie asks, 'Hey, Brent, if the Rapture happens and that receiver is a Christian, who would catch the ball?' So we had a chance to talk about the Rapture and the end times," Mitten said. "He really likes to talk about spiritual things. Just recognizing that some middle school students and high school students are still sensitive to spiritual things is always a blessing."

Staying the Course

In 1980, scandal shook the Boston Marathon. Rosie Ruiz crossed the finish line in record time and was proclaimed the female winner of the historic 26.2-mile race. But it would later be determined that Ruiz had not run the entire race. According to spectators, Ruiz entered the race at the twenty-five-mile mark. Marathon officials examined ten thousand race photographs and could not find Ruiz in a single one. The Boston Athletic Association disqualified Ruiz, and her designation as the female winner of the marathon was given to another. Today Ruiz is remembered as a cheat, one unworthy to wear the title "winner" because she didn't run the designated course.

There is much we can learn from this analogy as it relates to parenting African American youths. There are three key principles one learns in running this race:

1. Establish your trustworthiness.
2. Meet them where they are.
3. Provide them with an environment for continued growth, that environment being the church.

Trust is a key factor in building relationships with anyone, especially African American youths, many of whom have been abandoned by their fathers. Staying the course doesn't mean the mentor had to be there at the early stages of the child's life. But it does mean being consistent in your dealings with them and being willing to finish what you started. African American youths are looking for role models they can trust.

Mitten says that has been key in his relationship with urban youths. "At first I thought I'd be here for two years. Then I realized two years just wasn't going to cut it in terms of making a real impact on a group of young men," he says. "I started to understand what some of the pioneers in urban ministry were saying: that you need to be in it for the long haul in order to see the results of your work." In fact, Mitten says many inner-city youths refuse to commit to meaningful relationships because they have come to expect a sort of "here today, gone tomorrow" approach from everyone—Christians included.

Trust is always a big thing with any youth. There are always questions. *Who is this adult? What are you about? Why are you here, and when are you going to leave?* "My first year here," Mitten says, "the question I would be asked most often was, How long was I going to be here? I don't think it was a malicious type of question. They had seen so many people come and go they had come to expect it."

Trust isn't conferred based on the color of one's skin. "I automatically assumed, I'm African American. These are African American boys. Hey, I'll fit right in," Jackson says laughing. "But regardless of race, creed, and color, you've got to earn the trust of an individual. You have to earn the right to love somebody because they won't allow you to otherwise. They'll keep you shut out." Jackson began earning his "right to love" the teenage kids to whom he ministers by hanging out with them at school. Through a relationship with the principal of the high school, Jackson was able to visit on campus during school time. "I would go to lunch and sit and talk with some of the people there, and my face became familiar with a number of the students. They would speak, and I would speak, and I would start inviting them to come out to the Center and to church."

Hipps says Jackson employed another principle crucial to parenting and mentoring African American youths by interacting on their level and in their surroundings. "You've got to go where the kids are. You've got to meet them on their own turf, go to their games, go to their environments and their homes, not expecting to always meet them at church and church activities," Hipps says. "You've got to teach them how to live in their own environment."

Meeting the kids in their own environs is an important principle but one many ministries hoping to reach urban youths fail to embrace. Yet we see from God Himself this principle in operation in the birth of Jesus. The Center has taken that approach by locating its ministry within the community. Dr. John Perkins, founder of Voice of Calvary Ministries, teaches a philosophy of incarnational ministry, which is to live with the people, identifying with them.

But even though the Center has a presence in the community and has built its credibility with local residents, the local church provides the framework and structure for continued growth. Hipps, who has worked in urban ministry for nearly fifteen years, says he has witnessed the tragedy of a ministry not being properly linked to the church. He recalls a para-church ministry he worked with in the past. "We were working independent of the church," Hipps says. "We didn't connect to the community or any family structure at all. As a result, at the time I left, many kids either had nonexistent faith, were dead, or in jail. Working with youth ministry is not an end in itself. You've got to connect it to the greater life of the community, the church."

Setting the Pace

The difference between a sprint relay and a distance relay or even a cross-country marathon is that in a distance relay there is usually a pacesetter. The pacesetter is that runner who bolts out in front at the start of the race and gives the competition a speed at which to pace themselves. In the spiritual sense, Jesus is that pacesetter, the One who has set the standard for the race. It is through His approach that we find the way to set the pace in our ministries to young people. If we figure out the strategy Christ used and use the same strategy to develop our ministries, we can't help but be successful.

Effective ministries employ a balanced approach to evangelism, discipleship, and leadership. Most churches are one-sided. They are either good at evangelism, good at discipleship, or good at developing leaders. But they have to be good in all the areas. Evangelism is what brings people into the fold. Discipleship is the process of growing them up after they have come into the fold. Leadership development involves turning the ministry over to them so that they can have ownership of it and, in turn, start the process over again. We must visualize that process all the time.

It Takes Time

The principles and stories we have shared involve time, money, willpower, and much prayer. But as the national will turns toward finding solutions to parenting our youth and college students, we should adhere to these principles. Then

and only then will the nation realize how much hope there is
in parenting our young people.

---

*Rev. Gerald Austin, Sr., is founder of The Center for Urban Missions and pastor of The New City Church in Birmingham, Alabama. The Center seeks to help families move from dependency to true sufficiency by providing a wide range of spiritual, educational, and community development–oriented ministries. **William C. Singleton III** is a metro reporter for the* Birmingham (Ala.) Post-Herald. *He is a member of The New City Church and a volunteer for The Center for Urban Missions.*

Chapter 8

Evangelism

BY REV. DONALD CANTY, REV. DONOVAN E. CASE, REV. J. D. ELLIS, OWEN FRASER, REV. THOMAS FRITZ, CRAWFORD LORITTS, REV. PELLAM LOVE, REV. CHARLES OLIVER, TOM SKINNER, AND DEWAYNE TURNER

Before we begin an in-depth look at evangelism, it is important to define the term. There are many definitions of evangelism, and there are varying opinions on how evangelism should be accomplished. Let us begin our definition by saying that evangelism is part of a process. The Great Commission in Matthew 28 commands all Christians to evangelize. Evangelism involves

1. proclamation of the Gospel with the intent of conversion,
2. providing enough information for an intelligent decision, and
3. corporate fellowship.

Hence, we arrive at the following definition:

Evangelism is the presenting of the Good News of Jesus Christ's life, death, burial, and resurrection in both proclamation and lifestyle, so as to lead people to surrender to the lordship of Christ over their lives.

The Bible gives us a very clear picture of evangelism. The appeal to the unsaved came from all believers, not from just a select few. The Gospel was presented by both lifestyle and word of mouth. The motivation for evangelism was love for Christ and love for people.

In times past, the black church's perspective on evangelism has varied. Many have felt that evangelism was the annual revival. Not only did the saints reach out to the lost, but it was a time for spiritual growth and challenge for themselves as well. Others have viewed evangelism as an invitation to a church service or to a church-held program. Still others have felt that evangelism was what the church hired the pastor to do.

Purpose

Up to this point we have discussed what evangelism is. But definition is meaningless without purpose. What is the purpose of evangelism?

If we look at the big picture, the purpose of evangelism is quite simple—to build up the family of God (Romans 8:29). A closer look, on the other hand, shows us that becoming a family member involves more than simply being added to the family tree. We define the purpose of evangelism as follows:

The purpose of evangelism is to initiate people into the family of God and to transform them into vessels through whom Christ expresses Himself on the earth.

The Black Church and Evangelism

Historically speaking, the emphasis of the black church's evangelistic message was on quality of life and discipling the people (initiation). Believers were instructed to love God and people, including the oppressor, and encouraged to be what God wanted them to be. Around the 1920s and 1930s, the black church's perspective began to shift. Secularization of the black church occurred around this time as other black institutions began to emerge. The black church shifted its emphasis to the number of members rather than the quality of life. It became more concerned with affirmation (being accepted) than initiation, and with preservation rather than propagation (spreading).

This is not to say that the black church has not reached out. It has. But this trend toward preservation, toward maintenance rather than growth, reveals a profound lack of a sense of mission. And though the situation is improving, our lack of a sense of mission still remains. The black church must reach out farther than it ever has. The fact is that many black Christians do not realize that evangelism and discipling of blacks are primarily the responsibility of black people. Black Christians too often let white Christian institutions determine their spirituality. This self-imposed limitation holds back the black church. When it truly understands the purpose of evangelism, the black church will regain the passion it has lost for the spiritual dynamic of Christian leadership and the true meaning of weeping over lost souls.

Practical Models

It is our prayer that we have sufficiently communicated what evangelism is and its purpose. In the following pages we will share with you some effective methods and models used in evangelism. We find it convenient to divide evangelistic methods into five categories: mass evangelism, relational evangelism, confrontational/initiative evangelism, lifestyle evangelism, and need evangelism.

Mass evangelism. Mass evangelism, *the appeal to large groups of people*, is one method found in Scripture. It can be accomplished through crusades; revivals; some small group situations of, say, fifty people; and mass media.

Historically, the black church used several types of mass evangelism. One was the *religious emphasis week* on black college campuses. This was a student evangelistic outreach. Colleges like Morehouse and Spelman, which are dedicated to the training of black individuals, combined academics with religion. *Chapel* was a required assembly. The dean of chapel was the campus pastor.

Today, these ideals are being revived. Moreover, the dean of chapel is now more than a pastor on campus. He is also involved with the administration. The students who become involved in campus ministries usually go on to be a vital part of our local black churches.

Another type of mass evangelism was the *music revival.* Through this type of evangelism came the "mourners' bench," which was as significant to the conversion process as the preacher himself. The mourners' bench embodied a loving plea to sinners and prompted a proliferation of new hymns like "Sinner, Please Don't Let This Harvest Pass." The older Christian women and men rallied at the mourners' bench and worked with those seeking to find forgiveness and reconciliation.

The idea that a person could accept Christ as Savior and wait until later to acknowledge Him as Lord was foreign to the mourners' bench concept. The saints waited there with you until you had accepted a whole work of grace. Whenever someone was recommended for baptism, the mourners' bench workers would testify to that person's entrance into the kingdom of God.

Family reunions also served as a time for mass evangelism. This was perhaps the most highly anticipated opportunity for evangelism and was always centered around the church, with a service usually beginning the family activities. *Extended family evangelism* has followed the black church throughout its history. Usually the older family members proclaimed the Gospel, both through their words and through their lifestyles. They felt that blacks should lead the nation with exemplary spiritual commitment and social grace. They taught their young to love God, to work hard, and to be twice as good. This was a call to excellence! If evangelism is to be effective in the black community, it must work through the extended family. The black church should reclaim this part of its original heritage.

Some other historical occasions for mass evangelism included *tent meetings* and *funerals*.

Relational evangelism. Relational evangelism may come somewhat easier than the other four types being discussed. Blacks, for the most part, are a relational people, establishing personal contacts with business and work associates. Our definition of relational evangelism goes beyond getting to know people and establishing relationships. Relational evangelism is the *ability to win the right to be heard through serving.*

In times past, the church, the school, and all of the community functioned as part of a whole. Those with whom you went to school were the same friends you knew from church. The schoolteacher usually taught Sunday school. The school choir sang gospel because the teacher, no doubt, directed the church choir. The preacher had a six-day relationship with the congregation. All programs in the black church were relationship oriented, emphasizing a good self-concept. In short, relational evangelism integrated church and community.

Confrontational/Initiative evangelism. Most of our days are filled with people. We come into contact with people from various walks of life and in many different types of situations. The vast majority of the people we meet need to know Christ. We define confrontational/initiative evangelism as *confronting the varied people you meet every day as to their eternal state.*

This type of evangelism is hard because it is "cold turkey." No prior relationship or even knowledge of the person may be possible. You might not think yourself capable of this type of evangelism, but remember this very important fact: Evangelism is learned by doing! With time and experience, fears of evangelizing vanish.

Confrontational evangelism has always been a strong point of the elders and the mothers of the church. They confronted sinners with confidence and ease, not only at church, but wherever they found sinners in their midst.

In earlier days, evangelistic confrontation was usually black to black or white to white. Cross-racial evangelism was not common. From 1865 to 1914 the black church addressed black people, resulting in the most dramatic and explosive growth period in black church history. From 1914 through the mid-1950s, the black church reestablished itself. There was a search for identity and migration to the North. The birth of the independent black church movement occurred in 1950. When the black church focused on evangelism as a priority, the results were overwhelming. One thing we have learned from white evangelicals is the mistake of those who did not focus on evangelism as a priority in one generation, resulting in the failure to claim thousands of souls for the kingdom. Evangelism must be a priority.

Lifestyle evangelism. Every Christian can become deeply involved in lifestyle evangelism. There is no fear to overcome like that of confrontational evangelism. The size of your congregation is not relevant. Lifestyle evangelism involves *living in such a manner that your very life becomes a witness*. The irrefutable testimony of an effective walk with Christ is visible to others. Your behavior is so far from the norm of today that it intrigues others and prompts them to inquire about the reason for the difference in you.

There was a time when lifestyle evangelism was quite prevalent in the black church and community. The schoolteacher was a Christian and taught values and morality in school. There was a general respect for the church and for the Lord. Though the church did not have all the resources we are privileged to have today, it was still able to grow and produce God-fearing Christians. Lifestyle evangelism is a constant witness. It becomes so much a part of the individual that it is automatic.

Need evangelism. The last of our five categories of evangelism and perhaps the most recently developed, need evangelism, *combines the meeting of physical needs with the sharing of the Gospel*. It recognizes that it is hard for a hungry or sick person to respond to the Gospel. It is imperative that we meet people's needs in order to effectively minister to them. In more recent days, the black church has again become concerned with a more holistic evangelism. Many churches are now providing food, clothing, and shelter for those in need. Still others are providing counseling and day camp. With this meeting of needs, they also share Christ. This type of evangelism takes much work and careful planning. If we are genuinely concerned about others, the time invested is well worth the effort.

Methods

At this point, we list some effective methods and models that are currently being used across the United States.

- Counseling as an evangelistic tool
- Black male survey questionnaire
- Home evangelistic Bible study
- Door-to-door witnessing
- Home dinner party outreach
- Street meetings
- Block parties
- Spouse evangelism
- Men's (Women's) breakfasts
- Direct mail evangelism
- Youth activities
- Friendship evangelism

These are just a few of the successful methods being used today. No doubt your church has its own unique or even similar methods of evangelism. The idea is not necessarily to change your present methods, but to supplement those methods that are working well for you.

How-Tos

One of the main problems of evangelistic outreach is not so much lack of ability as it is lack of strategy and know-how.

In this section, we will provide you with some step-by-step how-tos of two kinds of outreach. If you do not have an effective outreach program, you might try one of these.

Home block parties. This type of block party takes place indoors, usually at the home of one of the saints in your congregation. The host must be friendly, outgoing, and hospitable, able to create an atmosphere which encourages friendships. The mood should be low key and casual. Invitations should be primarily to those not saved; but a certain number of saints, of course, are welcome and needed. Here are some things to include:

1. Start with icebreaking games. Example: Have persons say their names, where they are going, and how, repeating the initial letter in their names as often as possible. ("Sally, going to Senegal in a Sailboat.") Association will help others to remember your name.
2. Have a time of sharing. Ask, for example, "What was the most meaningful time in your life?"
3. Invite the unsaved into the family of God. Focus on Christ as the central issue.
4. Close out by
   a. having visitors sign a guest book or sheets (for follow-up and witness),
   b. praying for all the guests, and
   c. having the visitors drop their name tags in a box if interested in further fellowship.

Street block parties. This type of party takes place outdoors. It can be held on the church's block or on a congregation member's block. Here is what to do:

- Speak to residents of the block before making plans. This can be done via the block club president or door-to-door. If residents of the block object, you should make other plans. It is vital that the church maintain good relations in the community.

- Make sure you have received a permit from your local city government.
- Call in a carnival, musicians, and so forth, to provide games, prizes, and food.
- Close the block to prevent entrance by automobiles.
- Make sure that you have people competent to share the Gospel.

Resources Needed

Well-planned evangelistic thrusts require prior planning and a variety of resources, such as those listed in table 8.1.

Table 8.1
Resources for Evangelistic Outreach

Human Resources	Material Resources
Conceptual thinking	Information gathering systems (e.g., surveys)
Creative thinking	How-to materials
Leadership	Evangelistic materials (tracts, etc.)
Vocational skills	Gifts-in-kind (clothes, etc.)
Trained people	Charitable resources (soup kitchens, etc.)
Prayer	Equipment, audiovisuals, projectors, and facilities

While adequate resources are important for evangelism, let us be careful that we don't overlook prayer and dependency on God. Resources do not automatically guarantee God's blessing. Any work, big or small, relies upon God for true success.

Three things were important to Christ in His ministry. These attributes should be important to us, as well:

- An active prayer life

- An attitude of submission to the Holy Spirit
- Knowledge of the Scriptures

Now that we have some resources for accomplishing evangelism, how do we manage those resources for maximum effectiveness? One way is by using accepted principles of planning and administration in the work of the ministry. Too often the black church has labeled these principles as "worldly," not realizing that many of the concepts have their roots in Scripture. Much too often we use the blanket excuse, "I'm just going to trust God," without doing that which is essential for the furtherance of the ministry.

Planning, research, and the incorporation of change are essential parts of any ministry. Successful planning means there will be change. As change occurs, new planning must take place to accommodate it. The black church must begin to use these tools if it is to be successful in evangelism.

This chapter was developed by the authors at the first Summit of Black Church Leaders in Detroit, Michigan. Reprinted (with minor textual changes) from *Black Church Development* by permission of Parker Books.

Rev. Donald Canty is director of counseling for New Birth Baptist Church (Atlanta). Rev. Donovan E. Case is president of International Christian Ministries (Mo.). Rev. J. D. Ellis is National Evangelism Consultant (retired), Baptist Home Mission Board, Southern Baptist Convention. Mr. Owen Fraser is retired pastor of Bethany-Pembroke Chapel and a former member of the Board of Directors, William Tyndale College (Farmington Hills, Mich.). Rev. Thomas Fritz is National Coordinator, Intercultural Ministries, Campus Crusade for Christ. Mr. Crawford Loritts is a National Director for Campus Crusade for Christ. Rev. Pellam Love is pastor of River Rouge (Mich.) Bible Assembly. Rev. Charles Oliver is pastor of Elim Baptist Church (Detroit). Mr. Tom Skinner is the late president of Tom Skinner Associates. Mr. DeWayne Turner is director of Fishers of Men (Chicago).

Chapter 9

Discipleship

BY JOSEPH WHITE, RON BALLARD, ALAN CHAMBERS, HERMAN HEADE, DAVID JONES, GEORGE MOORE, MATTHEW PARKER, AND MELVIN UPCHURCH

There are all kinds of disciples—disciples of Marx, disciples of Freud, disciples in cults. Jim Jones's followers could have been called disciples. Then there are disciples of Jesus. In this chapter, we will look at what a disciple is and what the discipleship process involves.

Discipling is the process by which one person develops another by setting forth a philosophy and way of life. The disciple is called to take in the philosophy and follow the example of the discipler. As we mentioned, any philosophy or movement can have disciples. The Christian discipleship process is unique in that it starts with a commitment to Jesus Christ as both Savior (His death on the cross to reconcile man to Himself) and Lord (His leadership and authority in the life of the believer). No person can be a disciple or a discipler unless that dual commitment is in him or her.

Being a Christian means being a disciple. That means it is

not enough to be a person who attends church regularly, tithes, and is a "good worker." Some liberal Christians have done well in the social arena in concern for the poor and for justice, but often at the expense of personal spiritual growth in character according to principles contained in the Word of God.

Evangelical blacks, on the other hand, often err in the opposite direction by ignoring the larger community and concentrating on the spiritual integrity of the individual. What we need as a whole black church is a balance between individual spirituality and the broad issue of social justice. Acts gives a good picture of this kind of balance:

> And in those days, when the number of the disciples was multiplied, there arose a murmuring of the Grecians against the Hebrews, because their widows were neglected in the daily [serving]. Then the twelve called the multitude of the disciples unto them, and said, It is not [right] that we should leave the word of God, and serve tables. . . . [These] they set before the apostles: and when they had prayed, they laid their hands on them. And the word of God increased; and the number of the disciples multiplied in Jerusalem greatly; and a great company of the priests were obedient to the faith. (Acts 6:1–7)

The Christian discipleship process takes in many areas, as we have seen. But to boil it down to essentials, here is a general definition:

> The process by which a Christian with a life worth emulating commits himself or herself for an extended period of time to a few individuals who have been won to Christ.

Purpose

The ultimate purpose of any Christian endeavor should be to glorify God. Ephesians 1:12(NASB) says that "we who were the first to hope in Christ should be to the praise of His glory." The majesty of God causes us to stand in awe of Him and desire that He be made known, lifted up, and glorified.

Salvation was not instituted to make us comfortable. The

disciple should know that he or she can also glorify God in life or in death by receiving blessings or being made to suffer, or, as Paul puts it:

> I know how to get along with humble means, and I also know how to live in prosperity; in any and every circumstance I have learned the secret of being filled and going hungry, both of having abundance and suffering need. I can do all things through Him who strengthens me. (Philippians 4:12–13 NASB)

The human role in the discipleship process is found in two other passages:

> [For] the equipping of the saints for the work of service, to the building up of the body of Christ. . . . The things which you have heard from me in the presence of many witnesses, these entrust to faithful men who will be able to teach others also. (Ephesians 4:12 NASB; 2 Timothy 2:2 NASB)

The purpose of discipleship is to aid, guide, and equip Christians to do the work of the ministry and to reproduce themselves with the following goal in mind:

> [Until] we all attain to the unity of the faith, and of the knowledge of the Son of God, to a mature man, to the measure of the stature which belongs to the fulness of Christ. (Ephesians 4:13 NASB)

Role of the Pastor

The pastor can help promote a discipleship mentality in the church body by first developing faithful members, initiating the discipleship process himself, and then maintaining a support community of people committed to one another. Scripture highlights five areas of development:

- Equipping the church (Ephesians 4:7–16; 2 Peter 3:18)
- Disciplining the church (1 Corinthians 5:1–13; 2 Corinthians 2:1–11)

- Promoting *koinonia* (fellowship) in the church (Hebrews 10:24–25; Acts 2:41–47)
- Service in the church (Acts 6:1–7; 13:1–5)
- Elder oversight in the church (1 Peter 5:1–5)

Just a few words about this last point. The crucial role of elders and co-ministers has traditionally been neglected in the black church. It is important for the pastor to set lines of authority such that everyone is accountable to someone else, with the elders and younger ministers accountable to the pastor. God commands authority in four main areas: in the home in the parent/child and husband/wife relationships (Ephesians 5:22–23; 6:1–3); on the job between employers and employees (Ephesians 6:5–7); in society with civil officials (Romans 13:1–7); and, finally, in the church, with the elders (Hebrews 13:7).

It should not even be necessary to say that the accountability/authority process breaks down in the church if the elders and younger ministers are not in submission to God and His Word. The discipline process is only as strong as the discipler and the disciple. The church leadership must present a united front, saying what God says, and themselves growing in the Word. Perhaps the pastor could develop a leadership manual that communicates the philosophy of the church and the responsibilities of leadership. Titus 1:6–9; 2:1–10 is an excellent place to start.

A Few Tips for Disciplers

A discipler should have a gentle, caring disposition toward his disciples.

> But we proved to be gentle among you, as a nursing mother tenderly cares for her own children. Having thus a fond affection for you, we were well-pleased to impart to you not only the gospel of God but also our own lives, because you had become very dear to us. (1 Thessalonians 2:7–8 NASB)

Make sure you tailor the discipleship process to the

needs of the individual. Don't be so regimented that you neglect to discern where the person is in his or her development. Emphasize principles over methods, meeting needs over developing techniques, thought development over skill development, and trusting God over learning theories about God. Make sure you have an overall plan (being careful to be flexible) which includes short- and long-range goals. Start new Christians off with "milk" (1 Peter 2:2; 1 Corinthians 3:2) by emphasizing their security in Christ, teaching them how to pray, and starting them off in the book of John, for example. Remind them that their emotion or lack of emotion has no bearing on their position in Christ as a believer. Also, make sure they develop conviction (a strong sense of right and wrong) and a proper perspective on their relationship to God and to people both inside and outside the church.

Parachurch Organizations

Parachurch organizations are not churches, but groups that develop and implement evangelism/discipleship methods. It is important that we not mistake the parachurch for the church. The black church would do well to take a page from the book of parachurch groups. Some of their methods are valuable and can easily be transferred to a church discipleship program—but do not focus on the parachurch as the primary institution for discipleship.

Resources—What Do We Have?

The black church has much at its disposal to continue and improve upon the work of discipleship—the most important being faithful people with conviction and vision. Music is another, much overlooked resource. The right music minister can tailor a program that ties music into the pastor's message and prepares the congregation for worship. Music can teach, comfort, enliven, and cause God to be glorified in the members. It has the potential to bring about revival.

Sunday school and the development of Christian schools are crucial components of the discipleship process. Through these outlets teachers give the day-to-day how-tos of the

Christian life.

One of the strong points of the black church has been the extended family. Since God works through the family as well as through the church, we as believers should be thinking about how to minister to whole families. Some leaders are developing family seminars to address this need. This is one way to address the needs of young educated blacks, who are getting further and further away from the church.

There are black Christians all over the country with skills in each of these areas. For the black church to move on, it will have to begin the much-publicized process of networking, particularly across denominational lines. We have a lot to share with each other. It is our prayer that this book serves as a catalyst to allow this to happen.

In order to be an effective discipler, you must have a heart of love toward your disciples, time to spend with them, and a plan to help them—all under submission to the will of God through Jesus Christ and total dependence on the Holy Spirit to make your works effective.

This chapter was developed by the authors at the first Summit of Black Church Leaders in Detroit, Michigan. Reprinted (with minor textual changes) from *Black Church Development* by permission of Parker Books.

Joseph White is pastor of Mt. Lebanon-Strathmoor Church (Detroit). Ron Ballard pastors Home Ministries (Dayton, Ohio). Alan Chambers is on the staff of Children's Defense Fund (Washington, D. C.). Herman Heade (deceased) was youth pastor of Trinity Presbyterian Church (Va.). David Jones is a Christian and Missionary Alliance pastor (Ohio). George Moore is president of a foreign missions agency. Matthew Parker is president and founder of the Institute for Black Family Development (Southfield, Mich.). Melvin Upchurch is pastor of Community Bible Church (Grand Rapids).

Chapter 10

The Spiritual Development of Black College Students

BY DWIGHT GWINN

The black church must become the extended family for black college students while they are away at college and when they return home. The church must not only witness the Word to black college students, but the witness of deeds must accompany any viable, fruitful ministry. In part of a larger statement on judgment in Matthew 25:31–46, Christ said, "Inasmuch as ye have done it unto one of the least of these my brethren, ye have done it unto me" (v. 40). This passage so readily fits the context of black college students' striving to balance their spiritual, social, intellectual, physical, psychological, and moral lives at a time that many of them are for the first time without the comfort, closeness, and encouragement of their biological families. Here is where the black church has a tremendous opportunity to witness the love of Christ to college students.

Liberals and conservatives have argued for years about

the relevance of the Gospel message to the whole individual. The black church from its inception held in tension the whole Gospel versus the whole individual. It was the black church's philosophy of the whole Gospel to the whole person that held the black community together during times of turbulence and oppression. The extended black family and the church together held in tension the felt needs of black people and set in motion ministries to meet the needs of the whole black community. Evangelism was a natural within such a context. It was not until the nineteenth and twentieth centuries that conservative and liberal debates over identifying the Gospel message gained influence in the black church and community through the training of black leadership and became a substitute within many black churches for the whole Gospel to the whole individual.

It is at this critical juncture in the life of black college students that the whole Gospel concept must regain and maintain its influence to reach the whole person. Among the growing number of college-trained black young professionals are the future leaders of the black church and community. It is at this point in the development of these black future leaders that the black church must invest its dollars, time, energy, and programs to evangelize, train, and equip the next tier of promising young leaders. To do this, the black church must effect social, moral, intellectual, physical, and psychological development in the life of black college students that results in the spiritual transformation of the total person for the cause of Christ.

Their Social Development

Most black students have been socialized into the grassroots culture of the black community, except for those few whose parents lived in or near a predominantly white community and the children attended a predominantly white school. These students are often bicultural. However, the monocultured students, with little experience in the predominantly white culture, will most likely find themselves in cross-cultural settings of mostly white college students and staff. While there will often be a number of bicultured black students in the college setting, monocultured black students will at times be even more frustrated as a result of the presence of these apparent betrayers of black unity.

The black congregation that is to be successful in reaching and supporting black college students should start its outreach with these vital facts in mind. Any church that overlooks these points will not identify with the most critical issues facing most young black students. Culture, cultural change, and adaptation are not all bad; but the stress and tension that accompany environmental and cultural adjustment must be addressed in creative ways that support and encourage holistic development in the life of black students.

Jesus' appeal to the woman at the well allowed her to feel comfortable with herself and to overcome a strong focus on self so that she was able to perceive that the kingdom of God was being presented to her. Social attempts to reach black students must allow for the freedom of self-expression and discovery of biblical principles that guide students in truth discovery about their own feelings and contextual experiences encountered in the college setting. The ministries and churches that pay attention to the cultural stresses and social tensions black students experience and address those tensions from a biblical perspective will have the most success in reaching and equipping black college students for future leadership in the black community.

Their Moral Development

In order for black college students to move up the ladder of moral development, they must realize that they are a part of a larger community with a vested interest in their development. Students need to accept the fact that the day will come when they are to return on that investment made in their lives. Too many black college students are finding their way out of the black church and community in pursuit of personal gain and glory at the expense of the extended community. Dr. William H. Bentley once said that "one cannot know where they are going unless they know where they come from. To reject or deny one's past is to reject or deny a vital part of who one is."

Even God Himself is a God of history and works in and through His people throughout history. One's history is a vital part of God's working through and among one's people. Much wisdom is passed from generation to generation through the preservation of historical records. The Proverbs are full of wisdom and insights that press the importance of one's knowing and holding onto the lessons of past generations. The teachings of Proverbs can serve as a tutor into the maze of moral truth.

Timothy, through his extended family, was brought to salvation by the wisdom he discovered in learning the Word of God as he went through his developmental years (2 Timothy 3:14–17). When the black church stands in the place of the extended family in teaching life's lessons to college students, it must lead them to the realization that each generation stands on the shoulders of previous generations and that they have a moral, biblical obligation to invest in succeeding generations (2 Timothy 2:1–2). The black church must structure its outreach and ministries so that relevant application of the Word of God is made to college students so that they will acquire a commitment to give back to the community.

Their Intellectual Development

Many students come from neighborhood schools that are inferior to those of their college peers. The academic deficits some black college students experience create frustrations and tensions that need to be offset with support and encouragement. If most students are given the time and challenge to advance intellectually, they will. The church has the responsibility to reach out to and encourage black students to hang in there until their change comes.

While most colleges don't have black counselors who identify with black students' academic experiences, local black churches can serve as a haven for encouragement. Within black churches are many college graduates who can identify with the needs of these students (Romans 15:1; Luke

22:32) and can help them overcome academic stagnation and acquire high-tech skills. This invaluable resource of professional persons within the black church must be tapped and utilized to its fullest potential in meeting the needs of black college students. Special times and functions that bring these two groups together must become a part of the black church's ministry to black college students.

Their Physical Development

Most black college students are physically inclined and are readily involved in athletic activities on the college campus. Although this is an area where the black church will be less equipped to assist college students, it can still provide instruction in the areas of health, nutrition, hygiene, and stress management. Black college students are increasingly dependent upon controlled substances as an alternative to stress management as they deal with ambiguity, racism, and heavy workloads. Within the last ten years, the suicide rate among black college students has increased. The black church must be ready and able to minister the Gospel (Romans 1:16–17) to the physical needs of a growing number of students faced with the pressures of an ever rapidly changing high-tech society that desperately needs black leadership to become models of grace and faith for other youth who are losing hope on a daily basis.

Their Psychological Development

Many black college students think they are ready for the real world that faces them—until they are brought face-to-face with the challenge of peers who are better prepared. This can be a traumatizing experience for a student who discovers his or her lack of knowledge and experience of a global world in a setting where conversation and demands to produce rightfully do not apologize to the unknowledgeable or inexperienced.

This period of psychological development can be a very frustrating time for black college students, who feel the pressures of self-worth and the challenge of commitment to keep the faith to complete the course. It is at times like these that they need to be grounded in Scriptures that promote confidence and encouragement:

> Nothing is impossible with God. (Luke 1:37 NIV)
> We are more than conquerors through him who loved us. (Romans 8:37 NIV)
> Lean not on your own understanding. (Proverbs 3:5 NIV)
> The peace of God . . . transcends all understanding. (Philippians 4:7 NIV)
> We live by faith, not by sight. (2 Corinthians 5:7 NIV)

Here again the black church must be ready, willing, and able to compassionately reach out to these perplexed and, many times, exhausted students who are stretched to their last mile to muster enough inner strength to stay the course.

Their Spiritual Development

The black church has the unique opportunity to be the spiritual tutor to these young college people at a time in their lives that is the most perplexing. There is ample opportunity to share the love of Christ, not in a superficial way, but by being a real-life example to black youth during probably the most flexible and open period of their existence.

Most black students will have had some experience with the church because of its association within the dynamics of the black community. Although increasing numbers of black college students are now less connected with the church, there are still significant ties and relations in the past lives of these students. Many black college students will have had some connection with the church either directly or through some extended medium, but the reality and understanding of the spiritual significance of the Gospel message in the everyday life of the individual will need cultivation and the development of clarity. Although many black college students will have heard the message of Christ and possibly believed on Christ, their faith will need developing into a practical walk with Christ in their everyday context.

Others will have knowledge of the church and Christ but not true faith in Him. The black church has the privilege, because of the flexibility and change associated with the developmental years of the black college student, to have a profound impact upon the spiritual life and Gospel witness to black college students.

Conclusion

Many black churches have made a conscious decision to establish programs and appoint people to keep in touch with church and community members who leave for college. Recognizing the vulnerability and inexperience of these young people and the many obstacles they will face, these contacts are vital to helping students clarify their values during the turbulent years of late adolescence. Particularly for the student who attends a residential college many miles distant from his home, the church can be a vital complement to the family whose bonds may or may not be adequate for the distances involved.

Dwight Gwinn (Covert, Mich.) is a board member of the National Black Evangelical Association.

Chapter 11

Campus Ministry and Conferences Change Lives

BY REV. THOMAS FRITZ

Several years ago when I was involved in campus ministry at the Atlanta University Center, I knocked on the door of a Morehouse College freshman. As a part of our strategy to reach incoming students, we had distributed questionnaires to find those who were interested in spiritual things. This student had checked the boxes to indicate that he was saved and also interested in participating in a discovery group Bible study. It was encouraging to hear him share how he had become a Christian in Orlando, Florida, and about his involvement in his home church.

Vacation Away from the Heavenly

I didn't know how significant this visit was until he later told me how he had changed his intentions to experiment with a non-Christian lifestyle. He had wanted to see the other side and take a spiritual vacation from God for a season. What would have happened if I hadn't visited that September day? This young man became a key leader in the movement on campus, and many came to the Lord. They could see a difference in his life.

This Is a Harvest, Not a Playing Field

Another student could not handle life outside the boundaries provided by staying at home with parents and involvement in the local church. He got involved in drugs and sexual immorality. Convicted, he confessed his sins and asked for God's forgiveness. He tried to live right, but he just couldn't overcome the temptation. Finally, frustrated by the environment of drugs, pleasing his classmates, and the good-looking women at nearby Spelman College, he went to his hometown and enrolled in a Christian college.

This points out that we must aggressively minister to our young people. Just to see them participate in church activities, receive good grades, and get to college is not enough. Some of our Christian young people live like the world. They are involved in sexual immorality, drugs, theft, and gangs. Often they succumb to peer pressure. Many will eventually return to walking with Christ and involvement in church. They wait to return until they have trouble in their marriage, can't handle their children, or are deep in debt. That is a lot of wasted years and unnecessary struggle. It is critical that we lay a foundation for a lifelong commitment to Jesus Christ. That means more than keeping them out of trouble, but also equipping them to triumph in the long, hard journey of life.

One of the most encouraging ministries in our church is the youth ministry. In many ways they are leading the way in evangelism, prayer, and hunger for the Word of God. Why? Ministry became a priority. Prayer, planning, and providing resources have made a difference. The church invested in scholarship funds for them to attend the Impact Conference. Since the conference, the high school students have a realistic view of living the Christian life.

Sending Laborers into the Harvest

The Impact Conferences (held in Atlanta in 1991, 1994, and 1996) are making an impression both nationally and internationally. Our church ministry to youth has skyrocketed since then. Our youth are more equipped in evangelism and outreach than most of the adults in the congregation. At Impact on the day of outreach they visited homes, distributed boxes of love (meals), and saw fruit as some received Jesus Christ as Savior.

After the Impact 96 conference, a small group of students went on a short-term summer project to West Africa. The assignment given to them by the local African ministry leaders was to start a campus ministry at the local university. Four weeks later, the results were astonishing. More than one hundred had accepted Jesus Christ as Savior, and sixty-five students were involved in follow-up Bible study groups. Those sixty-five students became the nucleus of a campus movement dedicated to reaching the entire campus. One of the students has committed to returning to West Africa as soon as she finishes raising her funds.

Principles I Have Learned

Stay cool, not cold, on hot issues. Don't assume that our youth are spiritually immune to the wickedness of our culture, regardless of how spiritual they may seem. Since they are exposed and infected, a program of preventive medicine is needed for them to stay healthy. They, too, are potentially exposed to pornography on the Internet, music videos on cable television, and immoral teachings of tolerance in our public schools. In many cases the influences to wickedness are greater than the influences of the family and the church.

Close the gap on rap. Some church youth try to convince me that the Gangsta Rap (East Coast or West Coast) they are listening to is OK. But when I ask for the headphones from the CD player, they won't give them to me. By explaining that adults don't like rap, they hope that I will stop requesting to hear their music. After all, the music artists give thanks to Jesus Christ when they accept their awards on television, don't they?

Parents and youth workers, please become familiar with the lyrics of rap and other contemporary music. Get the names of the popular artists today (the list changes almost monthly). Go to the music store and read the cover of the CD or tape. Notice the warning about the lyrics. Expose young people to this information and discuss the effect of immoral lyrics on the morality of Christians. Share why this is sin. Don't think that I'm biased against rap. I enjoy listening to the ones with good, decent lyrics.

Biblical Wild Thing

One rainy night in Atlanta, a room on the campus of Spelman College was filled with more than three hundred students. The meeting was scheduled for seven o'clock, but students filled the room ahead of time. The rain didn't stop them from coming. What attracted them? The subject was "Wild Thing: Let's Talk About Sex." Pastor Haman Cross from Detroit shared for ninety minutes on the biblical perspective on sex, based on his book of the same title. After the talk, hundreds remained for a time of dialogue with the speaker. They asked serious questions and explored deep personal questions as speaking with a trusted friend.

Young people are seeking answers. They have become accustomed to Christians not confronting the issues. They don't know that the Bible has much to say about sex. It seems that safe sex as defined by our culture is hazardous. I will never forget that rainy night in Georgia, for many lives were changed.

Show and Tell

Youth are looking for more than mandates. They are looking for role models. "You can tell me what to do and what the Bible says, but can you show me what it looks like in the reality of this world?" They are looking for hope. What is wrong with some profanity in rap music, they ask, if it is all right for adults to listen to it on rental videos and cable television? What is the difference?

As parents and youth leaders, we must set the example of godly living. Watch their expressions when married couples show love and affection toward one another. It shows that happily married believers have more fun. Our actions speak louder than our voices.

Conferences and Retreats

Conferences such as Impact are dynamite opportunities for students to have life-changing encounters with the Savior and His plan for their lives. There are a number of regional and national conferences each year. Speakers and musicians are selected who have demonstrated that God speaks to youth through them. Churches that prefer to do so may plan their own conference by adapting a program from another conference. I recommend that several churches cosponsor such a local event in order to share the vision and to increase attendance.

Retreats are typically smaller in size and stress small group dialogue and/or entering into a more intimate relationship with the Lord. Each block of time on the program is introduced by a speaker, after which each person is encouraged —but not coerced—to participate. Such times of deep sharing help the individual and others to process questions that may have been submerged for months, if not years. Elsewhere in this book (chapter 6), Kitchen and Dickson have a helpful discussion on journaling and related topics that work very well in the context of a retreat.

Get a Vision for the Youth

Proverbs 29:18 says, "Where there is no vision, the people perish [or are unrestrained]." Vision can be defined as *a clear mental picture of a possible and desirable future imparted by God based upon His Word*. It helps us to think strategically and keeps us focused on the target.

What is the desirable image you see in the high school and college-aged person? What has God placed on your heart? Are you satisfied with the status quo, or are you driven by change? Take the time and dream. A good vision should be inspiring enough to attract followers.

I want to see youth become victorious in the battles of life and lead a new generation for the cause of Christ. They are the future laborers to go to the harvest as businesspersons, teachers, athletes, social workers, politicians, pastors, and missionaries. See them not only as youth *inspired* for change but as youth who are *instruments* of change.

Without a Vision, the Godly Legacy Perishes

As parents, we also need to have a vision for our youth. This requires sacrifice. At the very least, it requires a sacrifice of our time to spend with our family in prayer, Bible study, and just listening. There should be no safer haven than the family. But parents, this will not happen overnight. It takes time and sacrifice. It is worth all that you can give. Let us stop the endless cycle of broken marriages, bad relationships, defeat, and hopelessness.

Make Ministering to Youth a Priority

If ministering to youth is not a priority, it will never happen. Listen to the reasons that keep us from focusing our ministry to youth. *There are so little funds available. We're too busy now with all the other programs in the church. If we just had more volunteers. . . . Let us concentrate on meeting the needs of the tithers and major givers.*

Youth ministry does not just happen. It requires raising funds for scholarships to conferences and retreats. It requires getting volunteers to transport youth to various places. Most important, it requires time spent in prayer, planning, and dreaming.

Our church needed a plan and youth workers as well as budgeted funds. I prayed and believed. The Lord provided. Now I am praying for a full-time youth director. Next, I'm believing the Lord for a family life center for recreation to be used for ministering, not only for our youth but to our community as well.

Don't think that your work is finished when your young people attend college. Your work has just begun. They need more prayer and ministry than ever. Often the church and spiritual values will seem obsolete and irrelevant to real life. Go beyond the limits of your own college students. Develop a ministry to reach other college students. This type of ministry should be outreach oriented with a physical presence on the campus. Don't get comfortable with transporting students to and from the church services. Get training on how to equip these students to lead others to Jesus Christ and build disciples.

Develop Relationships with Youth

To gain entrance into their lives, take the initiative to listen to and dialogue with young people. Don't limit your thinking to an official church service. Expand it to inviting them over to the house or to a restaurant. Attend events at their school, provide tutoring, and give them advice about getting college scholarships.

Growing Is More Valuable Than Going

Do you hold the position that the busier you are the less likely you are to get into trouble? Give our youth as much to do as possible for the Lord. How often are our church youth programs evaluated on activities unrelated to goals? As parents, we often think that our children are achieving if they are involved in many activities. Piano lessons, sports, choir, scouts, and clubs are just a few. But it is more than *going*; it is *growing*. Activities should be designed to help achieve goals— not just keep youth busy. What are the goals you have for your high school or college students?

I remember helping my former pastor, John Price, with the youth at church bowling parties, swimming parties, and skating parties. It was a lot easier to invite young people from the community to join us. I had a lot of fun and so did the youth. But those events had a purpose, and that was to share the Gospel of Jesus Christ to all who attended. That was my first ministry in church as a college student. John had me share the message of salvation during the customary break designed for this. There was fellowship among the believers, but there was also the giving of the "right hand of fellowship" to new believers.

What is the purpose for the activities (lock-ins, youth Sunday, retreats, conferences, and youth or college choirs) your church sponsors? How are you directing the Sunday school classes and Bible studies to help the young people reach the goals you have established? How do you select the topics of discussions? What exposures will benefit their spiritual development? Think through equipping the youth for God's service.

A number of other principles have proven themselves to be effective during my years of working with youth. In brief, they are:

- Listen to the quiet under the shouts.
- Listen to the felt needs, inner needs, and root issues.
- Communicate in the language they can understand.
- Reach out evangelistically to youth, but also involve them in the process.
- Rely on the truth of the Word—do not tolerate the world.
- Challenge the youth to be real (don't play church) and reach out to them.
- Give them an eternal perspective.

Over and over in sermon and song we hear that the Lord will "make a way out of no way." That is true. Another helpful perspective is that the Lord has already made the way. Let us follow His way, and in no way will we get lost. Let us never lose sight that He is the Way, the Truth, and the Light.

Rev. Thomas Fritz (College Park, Ga.) is National Coordinator, Intercultural Ministries, Campus Crusade for Christ.

Chapter 12

Educating Our Youth

BY THOMAS FLEMMING

The writings of Carter G. Woodson, Benjamin E. Mays, and John Hope Franklin are known to many who search beyond the usual school and public library sources. It is difficult to find a full account of the contributions of women educators like Mary McLeod Bethune and Bessye J. Bearden (whose son, Romare Bearden, is known throughout the world for his creative art). The writings of Booker T. Washington combined education with economics, beginning with church school literacy and expanding to employment and business.

Historically, the African American church practiced an open-door policy. All attending were welcome to learn to read, write, and spell the Holy Scriptures. It was in church school that some of the earliest forms of retention skills were taught through the memorization of Scripture. Many young people learned about God as Creator through Genesis 1 and also through James Weldon Johnson's 1920 poem "Creation."

Becoming one who reads is *basic* to obtaining an education. One cannot start too early to build a good vocabulary, spoken and written. It is also important to understand how reading connects with the entire communications network. Some of the earliest kinds of education from our parents and other adults came via our being able to correctly follow instructions. With today's information highway constantly pouring out content of every sort, the church has a great challenge and opportunity to encourage the wisdom of Solomon:

> Listen to your father, who gave you life, and do not despise your mother when she is old. Buy the truth and do not sell it; get wisdom, discipline and understanding. (Proverbs 23:22–23 NIV)

Godly parents and other Christian family members set the foundation from the crib, before the first step is made off the curb!

The breakup of the family is happening throughout our nation, including well-to-do families as well as those that are unskilled and low income. The church is often the only place where young people can find acceptance, peace, and trust. As Christians, we are familiar with such promises as "Come to me, all you who are weary and burdened, and I will give you rest . . . for I am gentle and humble in heart, and you will find rest for your souls" (Matthew 11:28–29 NIV).

Words like *weary, burden, insult, anxiety*, and many others come together on college and university campuses. They intermingle with words like *achievement, failure, excellence*, and *disappointment*. They are found today in much of the debates surrounding diversity, competition, scholarship, and research.

The African American church can and must become part of the academic experience of both the high school and the college students within their charge. The home, the church, and the school combine to make up three of the most important parts of the K–12 developmental years. Like a geometric pie, each institution contributes a third to the life of young individuals, and spiritually they must overlap so as not to have any noticeable seams.

The majority of underachievement found today among elementary, middle, or high school students can be traced to a lack of discipline at home, a nonliterate or confused understanding of Holy Scriptures, or a disrespect of teachers' instructions. Problems in following directions often reveal an inability to hear and concentrate on what instructions are given. Failure to complete assignments on time is often the result of a habitual practice of doing important things shabbily and at the last minute.

Young people often demand others to "play fair." Yet they sometimes are hostile, angry, and aggressive when asked to do the same. Honesty and integrity must be a two-way street. The church is known for teaching and practicing such Christian qualities. No committed Christian should request or direct a young student to work hard at goal achievement if he or she cannot show the student how such hard work is related to success. The accomplishment may require expertise different from that familiar to the mentor, but the extra effort spent mastering tasks in a step-by-step process can be traced back to observable instances where an honest response was needed and received; where to tell the truth or act rightly might have meant personal loss, yet to the adult model integrity was more important than gain.

The saying "experience is the best teacher" is true. Experience can also provide some of the best stepping-stones for students willing to follow. Here one often finds the spiritual connection between teacher and student. An experienced teacher who has mastered the subject and has an excitement, a positive confidence, and a genuine humility in communicating knowledge will also communicate inspiration to student learners.

An important title for Jesus was "Teacher" (one able to communicate). A Christian has this skill available; all that is required is being willing and ready to use it. One who examines the scriptural references describing Jesus as teacher has the feeling of starting as a freshman and graduating four years later. That, in essence, is what the apostle Paul explained to Timothy, his impressionable young student. (Read the two instructional letters written to Timothy and count the number of times Paul gave directives.) This might have been Paul's instructional curriculum for Timothy and others (Philippians 2:19–20).

Paul's teacher was the Holy Spirit.

> This is what we speak, not in words taught us by human wisdom but in words taught by the Spirit, expressing spiritual truths in spiritual words. (1 Corinthians 2:13 NIV)

Taught in this passage is the same word used by Jesus: "It is written in the Prophets: 'They will all be taught by God.' Everyone who listens to the Father and learns from him comes to me" (John 6:45 NIV).

Notice the instructional vocabulary—*taught, listen, learn*. This language, in reality, is what academic achievement is all about.

When those responsible for instruction within the African American church simply value the student, without discrimination between "secular" and "Christian," then these holy learning centers will attract more young students and increase the possibility of influencing many in a positive direction.

The best cure for the weariness of distraction is fresh input from the Holy Spirit through human dialogue. The burden of inaccurate, sometimes false, instruction creates an anxiety of underachievement and failure. If this advice seems too much in the extreme, you may want to compare the daily information found on any television channel or radio station. You may want to stand at any news or magazine rack to understand why God's holy place and His sacred curriculum are so much more needed and rewarding.

The sacred Scriptures were completed nearly two thousand years ago but are yet able to stimulate, to invigorate, human intelligence today. The holy curriculum comprises a rich vocabulary. Reading, writing, and listening to a variety of interpretations, personal points of view, scholarly research-based revelation, and mystical and prophetic possibilities are all are parts of the sacred curriculum. For the church, this is an ongoing instructional curriculum requiring fresh lesson plans that feed both the intelligence and the heart. It is spiritual food, yet it fills both body and soul.

The challenge is for the African American church to embrace the high school and college youth of our communities. Various academic programs today have mentoring programs for young elementary and middle school students. The church should ask, How does one who does not believe in the value of learning for the excitement and reward of mastery mentor a student to want to obtain mastery? How can one nurture the reading of a complete book, cover to cover, if one himself has not read an entire book in a long time?

Nothing replaces reading; even the mastery of computer skills cannot be compared with the power and pleasure of having read the words of a talented and creative writer. One of the best experiences the church could offer is to have its young people read an author such as Dr. Ben Carson or Rita Dove; or someone like Dr. Jeremiah Wright or Dr. Susan Johnson Cook. Then the church should coordinate its calendar so that when these authors are in town they might have question-and-answer sessions with the young students. Maybe the writers would allow the sessions to be video- or audiotaped to be used when the young students read the book a second time.

This is not impossible. An inspiring teacher—guided and motivated by the Holy Spirit—could convince these developing young thinkers that the mind responds differently to familiar information to which one can relate. These youth are capable of learning in a more meaningful way as a result of the extra creativity introduced by the teacher.

In summary, those early African American educators reached out to young learners in the only place where healthy and positive instruction could be taught to them. The black church had an open-door policy toward anyone wanting to learn. Knowledge and instructions were not dispensed in a segregated manner. Girls were not discriminated from boys. The artist was encouraged as much as the scholar. The youth could learn as an apprentice to cook, to become a mechanic, or whatever the black community needed. The orator was a bit more highly prized, yet one would not want to compare the preacher to the midwife!

Jim Crowism segregation was an oppressive system. Even today racism, classism, and privilege blame many who are without opportunities. The African American church can return hope and restoration to places where drugs and despair reign. It will take courage and unselfish willingness to promote the gifts and talents found in most black congregations. It will take spiritual visionaries who establish short- and long-term goals and who are willing to include the empowering Good News regarding economics as well as other personal growth information.

One of Martin Luther King, Jr.'s, favorite songs was

If I can help somebody as I travel along . . .
If I can cheer somebody with a word or song . . .
If I can show somebody who is traveling wrong . . .
Then my living will not be in vain.

May the same be said of those of us who have been abundantly blessed with gifts from Him who is the Giver of all perfect gifts.

Related Reading

Franklin, John Hope (1994). *From Slavery to Freedom: A History of African-Americans*. 7th ed. New York: Knopf.

Low, Augustus, and Virgil A. Clift (1981). *Encyclopedia of Black America*. New York: Da Capo.

Mays, Benjamin (1971). *Born to Rebel: An Autobiography*. New York: Scribner.

Thompson, Frank Charles. (Ed.). *The Thompson Chain-Reference Bible, New International Version*. Indianapolis: Kirkbride Bible.

Wedin, Carolyn (1990). *Inheritors of the Spirit: Mary While Ovington and the Founding of the NAACP.* New York: John Wiley.

Woodson, Carter G. (1968). *The Education of the Negro Prior to 1861.* Salem, N. H.: Ayer.

Zodhiates, Spiros (1992). *New Testament: The Complete Word Study.* Iowa Falls, Ia.: World.

Thomas Flemming *is assistant to the provost, Eastern Michigan University (Ypsilanti, Mich.).*

Chapter 13

The Challenge of Contemporary Race Issues

BY RODNEY SISCO

The problem of the twentieth century is the problem of the color line—the relation of the darker to the lighter races of men in Asia and Africa, in America and the islands of the sea," W. E. B. Du Bois once said (1903, p. 10). Ethnicity (the analysis of ethnic groups) and racial and ethnic relations have been topics of discussion in scholarly and popular literature for a great deal of time. In the past few years there has been a resurgence of spoken, written, and audiovisual data on these topics. The social development, sociological grouping, economic movement, interpersonal relationships, physiological distinctions, religious movements, and participation in the workforce of ethnic minorities are just a few topics one could find by merely searching the most recent periodical shelf of any local library.

Understanding the unique peculiarities and profound distinctions of each group has consumed both the intellectual and general public. The discussion of the relationship of races to each other has provoked a great deal of thought. Three major metaphors give understanding to race relations. (1) The *Melting Pot* is the notion of immigrants from all over the world converging in America, fusing, and producing a new and better culture by combining the best of each of the parts. (2) *Anglo-conformity* is the systematic coercive de-emphasis and eventually removal of cultural distinctions due to the aligning of one's self to the dominant culture. (3) The *Salad Bowl* embodies the recognition of unmeltable ethnics who all interact with each other, creating a tenuous form of cultural pluralism. Sociologists would use the terms *amalgamation*, *assimilation*, and *accommodation*, respectively.

> [It] is evident that there has been a growth of ethnic awareness of a different genre in America, whether it expresses itself in the comfort that older ethnic groups can now feel when proclaiming their Old World heritage or in the troubled and troublesome abrasiveness of the long subjugated ethnic minorities searching for a status yet to be won. Both the achievers and the achieving . . . face the universal problem of searching for, finding and maintaining roots and tradition in face of the appeals of modernity and homogenized living in the burgeoning mass society. (Mindel, 1983, p. 3)

Though a great deal of discussion has been evident over the years, the virtue of maintaining a cultural pluralism has grown in popularity and seems to be the dominant model of race relations in America today. *Cultural pluralism*—common terminology for an accommodation model of race relations—entails the freedom to be "American," while at the same time retaining one's cultural heritage.

Culture Shock

In the fall of 1980, I left my home in West Philadelphia for a medium-sized Christian liberal arts college in the Midwest. I entered as one of four African American freshmen (out of a class of approximately 520); and one of seventeen undergraduate African American students (out of a campus population of approximately 2,200). Of the four who entered as freshmen, only two of us graduated. The campus statistics at that time predicted that of the seventeen enrolled students, only ten would graduate (a little over 50 percent). During this time I enjoyed myself thoroughly; and yet I noticed that there was beginning in me a change—a change that had at its core a new recognition of the African American experience in America and my part in that process.

My collegiate experience also included a change in the way I perceived the campus (and world) around me. In my first years, everything was OK. I experienced no racial incidents. I had worked very hard to be better than what I had accepted as the definition of a black man in America. In high school, I—being one of a few African American students— had worked hard to "fit in" to the norm of my school peers. These peers also became the social referent group for me because my goals (higher education, Christian living, doing well for me—not simply for the grades) were in direct conflict with the goals of many of my peers in the neighborhood.

To this end, I took on the social norms of my "new" referent group and strongly assimilated into the white middle class suburban subculture—a subculture that my college embodied. As time progressed in my latter college years, this assimilation grew less and less acceptable to me as the norm of interactions for me as an African American. To this end, I began a process of evaluation, reflecting on both my school and home experiences. As I grew, it became more and more clear to me that there are differing levels of identifying with one's ethnicity and with the social environment in which an individual lives. This chapter attempts to recognize some of the components of the developmental process and to encourage proactive thinking on the part of college personnel in creating environments that enhance the personal development of all its students, especially students of color.

Race, Culture, Ethnicity, and Racism

Though the terms used in discussing race and racial relations often have a variety of meanings, the central issue is that in order to understand the "peculiar treasures" of humanity, one must address the diversity of the people that make up said humanity. In order to provide a foundation for this discussion, it is necessary to define the terms *race, culture,* and *ethnicity.* These terms have varying definitions depending on one's field of study, but most definitions center around similar themes.

For the sake of this discussion, the terms are descriptive and are not value laden. The term *race* was used initially by anthropologists as a way to mark the distinctions among the subgroups of man. According to Johnson (1990, p. 41), "When applied to human beings, [race] has typically represented an assumption of shared genetic heritage among groups of human beings based on physical characteristics." The most common characteristics are skin color and the size of eyelids (larger eyelids among Asian peoples, usually referred to as slanted eyes).

The term *culture* represents "all of the forces and the processes which contribute to a discernible group of people . . . objectified into an abstract word. Culture represents all those activities which contribute to the cultivation of a group of people" (Lee, 1991, p. 67). Culture, then, is both the process and the setting (context) that embraces the behavior of the members. Culture defines aesthetics, philosophy, values, and beliefs.

Finally, the term *ethnicity* represents the interaction between culture and race, embracing some of the components of each. Lee summarizes ethnicity as

> a relatively recent concept used to interpret North American society. Probably to most, an ethnic group is a group besides one's own—"it is those other people who live over there." To social scientists, ethnicity is used to describe sub-groups delineated by a mixture of ideological, historical, and economic factors. (Lee, 1991, p. 73)

Ethnicity is the result of social development involving

inclusion by birth, but is also a distinct socializing process.

Culture, race, and ethnicity in America work within the social boundaries of race relations. The challenge of understanding contemporary race relations in this country requires at many levels an understanding of racism and the underpinnings of such an ideology on the average person of color in America on a daily basis. As a point of reference, consider the following excerpt from the Joint Consultation on Prejudice and Racism conducted by the National Association of Evangelicals and the National Black Evangelical Association:

> We affirm another conviction of our Judeo-Christian roots. As a consequence of a fall from the original created state, humanity shares a sin nature. One of the marks of this sin nature, prejudice, is distributed among the diverse parts of the whole humanity. This prejudice, rather than allowing a celebration of the diversity of our one humanity, causes the holders of prejudice to view those who are different as inferior. When one ethnic group is in a majority or power position, its group prejudices against those who are minorities or out of power are often manifested in racism. Racism is prejudice plus power. Racism is, therefore, an institutionalized expression of a controlling group's prejudices.

There were a variety of motives in the establishment of the United States as a nation. Woven throughout its history was a pattern of racism by the white-dominated society that involved the displacement and destruction of one race, the Native Americans, and the enslavement of yet another, the Africans.

Racism is a foundational sin of the United States, fueled initially by economic greed and the exploitation of human resources. It has corrupted the foundations, institutions, and cultural mores of this country; prevented formation of a true cultural democracy; and enslaved, impoverished, and oppressed people of color in the United States.

The concepts of ethnicity and racism in America are linked by social experience. Unless an individual has actively sought to transform his educational upbringing, he is racist in ideology. I am not making reference to the yelling of epitaphs, the burning of crosses, or the obvious public disdain for people of color, but rather to the pious subtlety of the advantages of a white-dominated society that entreats one to believe the superiority of the white race and inferiority of all others.

> Racism is a composite of ingrained perceptions, attitudes, and actions concerning a whole group of people—and therefore each member—based on the overt characteristics of that group. The underlying assumption is racial superiority. So blacks have been perceived as inferior, which has justified attitudes of superiority and led to acts of domination and injustice. (Gross, 1985, p. 3)

Before the 1960s many Jim Crow laws required people to be and act racist. The South practiced systematic segregation. Northerners declared how bad this practice was while maintaining social segregation of people of color. Such are examples of the systemic and systematic encouragement of the beliefs of inferiority while at the same time stating many nice things about people of ethnic minority status.

For the most part, educational systems excluded from their curricula (and from photographs or content) any information regarding peoples from non-European backgrounds except when they referred to poverty and deviancy. In short, if the cultural norm is based on one group, all other groups are considered abnormal. This influences people on both a macro- and a micro-level, that is, from the societal to the personal. Table 13.1 reviews these levels.

Table 13.1
Levels of Influence

Cultural	Institutional	Individual
Aesthetics	Labor	Attitudes
Religion	Legal	Behaviors
Music	Health	Socialization
Philosophy	Educational	Self-interest
Values	Political	
Needs	Housing	
Beliefs	Church	
Theology		

Source: Brandt, 1991

Education and Ethnicity

Of the many institutions in our society, education has had the role of socializing young men and women into functioning participants within the society by introducing students to ideas and skills (physical as well as social) necessary for successful entry and proliferation. In America, the challenge of education is to create an environment conducive to the holistic development of all students. Unfortunately, many components of American society have not embraced a perspective that allows for discussion of the varying cultures and subcultures interacting in this increasingly pluralistic country. Many members of this nation are unaware of the positive attributes of various cultural groups. The academy must provide an environment that will allow for the healthy development of competent members of society who are aware of themselves and their ability to impact the world around them.

College is a chance to try on an assortment of new roles. It serves as a fertile ground for relationships and experiences that help one find out more about one's self. New experiences and the spurring onward of the developing cognitive, psychosocial, moral, spiritual, and other abilities are all part of the joys and pains of the college years. The college years have the frustration of developing a sense of intimacy with those around—or a sort of interpersonal isolation, as Erickson would maintain. Throughout this time, young adults search for people and ideas to believe in, decide on opportunities to become involved in, and seek to identify and prepare for a career they hope to find rewarding. In short, college is the environment in which young adults begin to feel out the path of not only who they are but also of who they will be.

Institutions of higher education face increasing numbers of ethnic minority students. This raises issues concerning such items as curriculum reorganization, campus organizations, and the need for minority faculty. These issues challenge and reveal inadequacies in the present system. On most college campuses, Anglo Americans outnumber ethnic minorities. The college experience is an important life transition, often compounded for the ethnic minority student entering a largely white student population (Ethier, 430).

Kunjufu (1990) and Wilson (1990) define the importance in the development of black youth of a strong sense of pride in themselves and their people—simply a positive self-image. Kunjufu identifies that most educational systems do not affirm black youth, but rather systematically reject them. This rejection can lead to the crippling (if not destruction) of a positive self-identity, which makes being a member of a minority group a negative concept. Both authors maintain that for black youth to develop a healthy and inclusive self-concept they need to know their own heritage. Knowledge of one's own heritage and equal appreciation of others' backgrounds make room for a healthy concept of one's self.

Christian colleges and universities struggle with these issues as well. Many are currently beginning efforts to attempt campus diversification, while a few have wrestled with these issues for some time. Unfortunately, being a Christian institution does not make a college void of racial tension. Boivin et al. attempted to find if any difference existed in racial prejudice among Christian and non-Christian college students. There was a significant difference between the profession of Christian faith in the Christian and non-Christian college student groups, as was expected. There was, however, no differ-ence in the scores on the racial attitude tests. The overarching emphasis appears to be that there is no relation of faith to maintaining inferior views of differing ethnic groups.

It has been this author's observation that students of col-or have a tendency to respond in differing ways on the cam-puses of Christian colleges where they are a distinct social and political minority. These observations have been summarized and categorized by Pollard, who has identified four basic mi-nority student coping strategies on predominantly white col-lege and university campuses. These actions reflect the various stages of traditional culture shock for some and are summarized in Tables 13.2 and 13.3.

Table 13.2
Minority Student Coping Strategies

Withdrawal, apathy, or depression
Separation, anger, hostility, or conflict
Assimilation—efforts to "fit in"
Affirmation—self-acceptance, positive ethnic identification

Source: Pollard, 1992

Table 13.3
Stages of Culture Shock

Initial Confrontation
Adjustment
Crisis
Honeymoon

Source: Pollard, 1992

The Value and Power of Education

There are a few insights that churches and parachurch ministries might keep in mind regarding the success and de-velopment of African American students in higher education:

• The backdrop of contemporary society and the discussion of race and race relations

- The socio-dynamics of the college setting and the challenges that young adults wrestle with as they engage in
the college life

The prophet Zephaniah wrote during a time when the
destruction of Jerusalem was imminent. Yet the reminder he
gave was that "the Lord, your God, is in your midst, a warrior
who gives victory; he will rejoice over you with gladness, he
will renew you in His love" (Zephaniah 3:17 NRSV). The same
admonition is the starting point as we conclude this chapter.

The continuing challenge is to remind our youth of the
power and value of their education. First, the test is for the elders of the church, specifically the men, to model their own
continuing goals of personal growth and achievement. Second, completing degrees through varied programs (traditional, extension, alternative credit for life experiences) reflects
our sacrifice and determination and ensures our ability to em-
pathize with our students. Finally, students need to be challenged to develop high goals that prepare them for a broad
cross-section of opportunities. Students need viable alterna-
tives to the competition of quick money either legally (sports)
or illegally (drugs, weapons, gambling). They need to recognize that they are preparing for life. Dr. Jawanza Kunjufu reflects this as he describes the difference in preparation
resulting from one's philosophical perspective. Table 13.4 reflects this difference.

Table 13.4
Goals of Educational Preparation

Educated	Trained
Employer	Employee
Career	Job
Analyze/think	Memorize
Life-long learning	School year learning

Source: Kunjufu, 1984

Both points of view have their merit. Yet preparing youth for the twenty-first century requires that a mind-set of excellence and determination settle in. This mind-set is best facilitated by the educated point of view. The educated youth is prepared to handle the multiple tasks with which society will challenge him or her while focusing on both personal and communal growth and development.

The college years provide an opportunity to wrestle with the foundations of all facets of life. As mentioned earlier, students of color in predominantly white college settings struggle with models of interaction with students from the dominant population. On the historically black college or university campus, this struggle is significantly relieved and the balance issue becomes one of encouraging knowledge of other ethnic groups as well.

Regardless of the campus setting (state university, community college, Christian college, black college), the student needs to focus on success in addressing the multiplicity of issues that will arise. Thinking must begin about responding to the roommate or peer who maintains and uses illegal substances in the room, the roommate who habitually abuses alcohol, the peer who consistently cheats in class work, or the roommate who leads an active sexual life (possibly with both sexes).

In any circumstance, students need to be prepared regarding both their spiritual foundation and their focus on excellence. The focus on Christ and excellence is the paradigm shift from the multiple influences in their lives that impact their inability to move forward. As discussed earlier, there are divergent forces in this nation that focus the student's point of view on the negative impact of African Americans. The church that prepares its youth for college can give the input they will need to address the assumptions.

Excellence. For your youth in college, there are a series of practical ideas to keep in mind. First, *excellence in sports can be equaled in the classroom.* Never let any faculty member (high school or college) convince you that you cannot do a subject. One subject may require more work and preparation than another, but it is possible to learn anything known to man.

In the event of overwhelming academic challenges, identify early the campus resources that are available to you. There may be an office of Cultural Diversity, Minority Affairs, or Multicultural Concerns that exists to support students of color. The only stigma to fear in capitalizing on the available assistance is failure if you neglect to avail yourself of the resources that are there for the asking.

Academic excellence is not limited to a 3.75 grade point average. Students need to push themselves beyond *normal* and strive to learn for the sake of personal growth, not for grades alone. Practically speaking, this means budgeting one's time so that one can complete all the reading and then review the reading and class notes at a later date. Repetition is key in the learning process. Study groups are among the best resources that enforce structured review of material. Study groups require that students will have done the preparation before they get to the group so that the time together can be used to develop new insights into the material at hand.

At the beginning of the school term, the student needs to examine the syllabi (course schedules and expectations) to determine when the crunch times are going to come in the term. Then they can plan a schedule for balancing time for achieving maximum, balanced effectiveness for studying for each class while allowing for relaxation, worship, service, and other creative pursuits. The general recommendation is two to three hours of study each week for every hour of class. In the selection of classes, the question should not be which require the least amount of work, but rather, what extra research can be done in areas of the students' interest.

Let me conclude these thoughts on academic excellence with the story of Debbie (not her real name), who was determined to major in biology. Unfortunately, although she had done well in high school, she quickly became aware that her high school preparation was significantly deficient compared to many of her peers. Thus, what many students had learned in high school was new to her in college.

Determined to achieve excellence and not appear *dumb*, Debbie asked the professor to meet with her once a week for forty-five minutes to review her progress. In class, while the professor lectured, she wrote down unfamiliar words phonetically and looked them up later. In the class reading, she used similar habits for increasing her vocabulary by studying difficult terms and related concepts. She utilized study groups from the Office of Minority Affairs as well as challenged herself to critical analysis (thinking the concepts through in relation to other concepts studied) instead of memorization only. Debbie did not graduate magna cum laude, but she graduated having mastered the biology major.

Spiritual development. The second area of concern for students is actually the first issue for growth. *The intentional effort of the student to maintain his or her spiritual development will influence his or her ability to manage the college experience.* Many students in college ask questions of their faith that they have previously ignored. For many, this is the time when they internalize their faith. Thus the role of the church is to provide them with a base that is scriptural, challenging them to seek the Lord fully.

When they return home for vacations, students should be actively encouraged to discuss the areas where they have grown. Equally important, they should be encouraged to choose a church home for the college years and to actively involve themselves there rather than hopping from one church to another. Looking for other churches within your denomination that have congregations near campus may ease this process.

Students need to be reminded that they will interact with many who call the name of Christ, who yet have very divergent Christian experiences. A student approached me saying that "none of [her peers at the Christian college] were Christians" because they "read" their prayers in chapel as opposed to being able to pray "in season and out of season." As we spoke, she came to understand that some denominations encourage excellence in presentation to the Lord; so the students she observed may have spent a great deal of time praying in private in preparation for the corporate prayer.

Students may ask new questions of their faith. This is all the more reason they need to know that they have a home that is going to point out scriptural truth and yet allow them to wrestle with questions of doctrine as they establish their faith for themselves. *And this is key.* They must determine the importance of their faith for themselves and do this in a manner that is supportive of their personal journey.

Heritage. A third area of discussion for success in college concerns the importance of the social self. Du Bois spoke of the double consciousness—that sense of being thoroughly multicultural. *Our students need to know the distinct joy and heritage that they come from in their families, church, community, and people.* That knowledge is in tension with the dominant culture in which they must survive. Knowledge of the past helps provide a foundation and hope for the future. The church should provide the foundation of understanding their cultural history so that they are prepared for the many who will define their faith as the *white man's religion.*

A healthy view of their ethnicity that allows for their faith to impact their outlook will ensure that they will be able to counter the cultural and institutional racism of the day with a sense of Holy Spirit–reinforced cultural pride. As students grow in knowledge of their cultural heritage, they should be able to relate with strength to individuals from other cultural backgrounds, whether they be other ethnic minorities or the dominant population.

Practically, students will have the opportunity to study courses such as African American literature, African American theology, African American politics, and so forth; as well as broader courses, such as racial and ethnic relations. This latter course offering helps to develop a broader understanding of other ethnic groups. Focus on one's ethnicity does not translate into exclusion from the dominant population. Students of color should be equally intentional to develop relationships with people who differ from themselves. This interaction develops a multiethnic consciousness, allowing us to communicate and understand people from multiple backgrounds.

Successful people of God can communicate His love across cultural lines, yet know their own cultural and spiritual heritage. This will have been enhanced by both the study of cultures and the development of genuine relationships. Ethnicity is not the only challenge of the college experience on the personal level. The confluence of ideas, beliefs, and perspectives might drive one crazy. Students need to be prepared to deal with issues of sexuality (I am referencing a distinct heterosexual paradigm as normative); the use or non-use of alcohol and tobacco; issues of their integrity; issues of supporting others; and keeping their schedule while they work, to name a few.

The social self is the combination of all the areas of the college experience outside the classroom. Students should consider the resources available to them in the many individuals on campus and off who want to see them succeed.

Maturity and Balance

Among the final things to remember for students in college is the fact that there are new challenges that will arise in their lives simply because they are continuing to mature. They will have to address issues regarding peers who make bad decisions; the ramifications of their own poor decisions; and striving to make sense of the world around them. They must seek to balance their physical needs (rest, food, exercise) with their social needs (ethnicity, dating, self-identity, mentoring younger students) and their spiritual needs (fellowship, scriptural reflection, prayer). The interaction of these multiple areas must be addressed in their church homes.

Our churches and ministries must provide the foundation for modeling this balance. What are you doing in your ministry to empower these youth? Encourage youth to pursue classes in high school that stimulate critical thinking. If the school fails to create community debate leagues, the church must create a forum where students learn to evaluate contemporary problems and determine excellent solutions.

Church workshops on values training should articulate

that flipping burgers is OK for a time; that money should be a reward for honest work. In short, the church should promote the notion that the family is more powerful than gang pressure.

Dianne (not her real name) approached me, believing that she was insignificant. During her four years of college, no man had asked her for a date. She also had poor study habits. Thus she felt she could not handle the academic pressure. She rarely had dialogue with other African American students regarding issues of culture and diversity. She felt that her self-worth was not being affirmed by so-called Christians in the arts (where she excelled). Eventually, she dropped out of college to pursue a relationship with a Muslim and perform in the arts. In short, she was a student whose networks were insufficient to keep her happy.

Remind students that the transition from high school to college is very difficult. Provide opportunities for them to internalize their faith by creating a Jr. Sermon Sunday where some of the youth who have been mentored by adults in the church speak. Develop a rite-of-passage program that marks the transition from one level to the next (see Sheldon Nix, *Let the Journey Begin*, 1996). Let students help in the development of the program. Develop a church library with information on various colleges and universities.

These are the beginnings of ideas of ways your church can prepare youth for college. The job is to prepare students for the multiplicity of issues they will face during their college years.

Conclusion

This chapter began with an analysis of contemporary race issues and the challenge they provide for the college student of color. Discussion moved to the unique tasks in college for students, concluding with brief examples of excellence. The goal is to have women and men from our congregations graduate from college confident of their gifts and able to use their talents to serve the Lord more fully. The expectation is that—though they may go through some form of initial shock in some settings—they will be empowered by their home church to affirm their own identity and become people of purpose who work from a concept of shared strength and creativity.

Their excellence in education—balancing all the challenges that the college years provide while maintaining their faith and distinct relationship to their community—is the end we have in mind. That communal relationship may involve their transforming their community by their example.

I end with one final student, Adam (not his real name). Throughout his college years, Adam actively attended to issues of his ethnicity. He participated in the black student union, sang in the gospel choir, studied with other students, remained in contact with his family at home (and church), and created student organizations. He also developed genuine relationships with students of Korean American, East Indian, Caucasian, and African American descent, and mentored incoming freshmen, helping them to acclimate to the college campus.

As an alumnus, Adam has maintained contact with the institutions while serving in ministry and public policy capacities. Adam was challenged to seek his faith fully even though there were those who sought to disrupt his college experience. Some professors made comments that were discouraging at best. Adam actively serves the Lord expectant of the twenty-first century even while addressing the current cultural challenge of multilevel racism. Adam remains faithful to his Lord in all areas of life and thanks the Lord for the gift of his ethnicity.

May our churches be places of impact that prepare students for the challenges outlined in this chapter, and more, while preparing for excellence in their lives.

Resources

Boivin, Michael J., Harold W. Darling, and Terry W. Darling. (1987). "Racial Prejudice Among Christian and Non-Christian College Students." *Journal of Psychology and Theology*, 15 (1), 47–56.

Brandt, Joseph. (1991). *Dismantling Racism: The Continuing Challenge to White America*. Minneapolis: Augsburg.

Du Bois, William E. B. (1903). *The Souls of Black Folk*. New York: Bantam.

Ethier, Kathleen, and Kay Deaux. (1990). "Hispanics in Ivy: Assessing Identity and Perceived Threat." *Sex Roles*, 22 (7/8), 427–440.

Gross, Bobby. (1985). "Racism with a Smile." *HIS*, 45 (5), 1–4.

Johnson, Samuel D. (1990). "Toward Clarifying Culture, Race, and Ethnicity in the Context of Multicultural Counseling." *Journal of Multicultural Counseling and Development*, 18 (1), 41–50.

Kunjufu, Jawanza. (1984). *Developing Positive Self-Images and Discipline in Black Children*. Chicago: African-American Images.

Kunjufu, Jawanza. (1990). *Countering the Conspiracy to Destroy Black Boys*. Vol. 3. Chicago: African-American Images.

Lee, John D., Alvaro L. Nieves, and Henry L. Allen. (Eds.) (1991). *Ethnic-Minorities and Evangelical Christian Colleges*. Lanham, Maryland: Univ. Press of America.

Mindel, Charles, and Robert W. Rabenstein. (Eds.) (1983). *Ethnic Families in America: Patterns and Variations*. New York: Elsevier Science.

Nix, Sheldon D., and Eugene Seals. (Ed.). (1996). *Becoming Effective Fathers and Mentors*. Colorado Springs, Colo.: Cook.

———. *Let the Journey Begin*. Colorado Springs, Colo.: Cook.

———. *Let the Journey Begin—Boy's Activity Book*. Colorado Springs, Colo.: Cook.

Pollard, Merriette. (1992). "Retention of Minority Students: A Model Program Utilizing Creative Untapped Resources." E.R.I.C. 234–669.

Wilson, Amos N. (1980). *The Developmental Psychology of the Black Child*. New York: Africana Research.

Rodney Sisco is director of minority affairs, Wheaton (Ill.) College .

Chapter 14

Day Care Evangelism

BY PHYLLIS SIDERS

There is no God apart from the Lord. "I am the Lord, and there is no other," the Lord proclaims. "There is no other God besides Me, a just God and a Savior; there is none besides Me. Look to Me, and be saved, all you ends of the earth! For I am God, and there is no other. I have sworn by Myself; . . . that to Me every knee shall bow, every tongue shall take an oath" (Isaiah 45:5, 21–23 NKJV).

Because there is no God but God, evangelism is a priority. Evangelism is preaching the Gospel to a dying world. We participate in the plan of God when we seek the lost. It is then that we are obedient to the command of Christ to go "into all the world, and preach the gospel" (Mark 16:15).

Looking for a model of evangelism that could be applied to the day care/preschool level, I went to Scripture and reviewed the example of Jesus. From that examination, it became clear that we need a sense of urgency in telling a dying world that God is love. If the church is to be responsible in discharging its God-given ministry to the community today, we must minister to children, both inside and outside the church. In addition, a broad review of Jesus' approach to ministry revealed that one cannot do evangelism without meeting the physical, social, and spiritual needs of children. The church must equip the children to become peer role models. We must teach them to give and support each other in times of need. I have taken these insights seriously as I have developed our program at School of Preparation.

Living in the 'Hood

At their tender ages, preschool children's problems tend to emanate from their family settings more than from the larger society. Especially in urban areas, family insecurity, family breakdown, violence, and fear often mark children's lives. A large number of children find themselves in families who never go near a church on Sunday or any other day. Hence, their problem-solving options are reduced. The children who come to School of Preparation Child Development come with little or no knowledge of Jesus. So this is our mission field.

At the same time, the church is often too busy looking at itself and drumming up support for its internal programs that it sometimes appears that we have forgotten the world. Children are a people in pilgrimage, for the most part, who remain largely unaddressed by people of biblical faith. No matter how modern, how urban, how technologically advanced, the heart of man remains the same, alienated from God. The Good News is still our critical need. This is true of children also. As Bill Cosby might say, we all "started out as children."

Developing Minds for Action

We can be more effective in telling the story of Jesus when we understand the other stories by which children are living. Stories are a large part of the way culture and values are transmitted to children as they are socialized into becoming adults.

The church should look at where the children are. There

is a large population in day care (including preschool centers and community programs). The day care center, then, could be a main focus for developing an evangelism program that can reach children on their level. The church needs to be willing to conduct regular programs at the day care centers that are receptive.

What Children Already Know

An assessment, or background check, of each child will provide valuable information for tailoring our approach to better serve the children. We need to know as much as possible about each child so that we can build a positive relationship with the child. An informed approach provides better opportunity for effectiveness.

Example—As You Are

One example of a day care/community program that we use is as follows. Children are worked with in groups of five. At the beginning of each session, a story is read from the Bible or a Christian magazine as a motivator and to help the children become more familiar with Jesus Christ. We teach the love of God from passages such as John 3:16. Teachers use a felt board for character and relationship building. The children appreciate the stories when presented at their level.

Telling a Friend About Another Friend (Telling Their Friend About Jesus)

Other techniques and examples include the following:

- Use a leading question, such as "When is the last time you shared a good thing with a friend?" (based on John 4:4–24). A creative teacher can do a lot with that one.
- Subscribe to a children's evangelism magazine. Read articles aloud to the students and engage their little minds in dialogue related to the article.
- Use calendar designs and cartoons to tell of the love of God.
- Music is a wonderful way to help children learn and re-

member information. Children naturally respond to rhythm and delightful lyrics.

Training for Workers

Children's workers must be trained in evangelism so that they can minister to children effectively. Over the past seven years, we have worked with over eight hundred children at School of Preparation Child Development, a preschool for children two and a half to five years of age. The preschool setting gives us a built-in group of children for evangelism. We have a Bible Time every morning.

Each day is started with a story of the love of Jesus. and the children are given an opportunity to accept Jesus as Lord and Savior. Our holiday seasons are built around the love of Jesus.

It goes without saying that day care workers need prior and ongoing training in their chosen field of work. In addition, I cannot overstate the need for training the day care workers who are to be part of the evangelism effort. Some persons have a knack for evangelizing children. Others need varying degrees of in-service training in order to be effective. The teachers in our school have been trained in evangelism and do a very good job of sharing the Gospel. Our basic training module consists of two sessions:

Session 1: The characteristics of preschool children
Session 2: How to reach preschool children with the
Gospel

After the training sessions, we recommend that teachers establish a regular time on a given day of the week to work with the children regarding the love of Jesus.

Conclusion

As the church moves into the new millennium, we must seek to reconcile lost people to God through Jesus Christ. As we do, we will feel God's pleasure because we will be doing what Christ has commanded us in Mark 16:15. That is to go "into all the world and preach the gospel." If what we say about Jesus is offensive or rejected by the hearer, we must know that it is not we who are being rejected, but the Stone the builders rejected in Mark 12:10.

It's a must that all of us become actively involved in God's ministry of evangelism.

————————————

Phyllis Siders is founder and president of SOP Family Services (Detroit).

Chapter 15

Building a Youth Ministry That Works

BY DENNIS TALBERT

National statistics indicate that over 80 percent of all Christians make a commitment to Christ before their eighteenth birthday. If Madison Avenue were looking at reaching this population, advertising and marketing agencies would be scrambling to get a leg up on shaping the minds of young men and women during their most impressionable teenage years.

Yet, in most urban churches, this group is often neglected or overlooked in hope of reaching a more mature group. Something is wrong with this equation. From a marketing perspective, these individuals represent almost a third of the expendable dollars entering the global economy. In real terms, that represents several billion dollars, equivalent to being the seventh largest economy in the world. In spiritual terms, reaching this population could represent exposing 100 percent of the African American population to the Gospel of Jesus Christ before the year 2010. With these simple numbers alone, it is time that we reevaluate how we minister to our teenagers in the African American community.

Solomon, the wisest man ever to live, said in a letter to his son, "Where there is no vision, the people perish" (Proverbs 29:18 PHILLIPS). And David said, "Each generation will announce to the next your wonderful and powerful deeds" (Psalms 145:4 PHILLIPS). Who will provide the vision today and who will announce the wonderful deeds of Jesus Christ to the teenage community?

How is it that in a society that is moving forward with great technological advances, the dropout rate in most major city's urban communities is averaging more than 40 percent between the ninth and the twelfth grades? How is it that our families are crumbling right before our eyes, even as everyone around us is quoting the African proverb "It takes a village to raise a child"? Perhaps the answer is quite simple. We've lost our vision for our youth and subsequently have stopped announcing to the next generation the wonderful deeds of our God.

While the church flounders in this area, the world (Madison Avenue) is actively moving forward to shape the minds of African American teenagers. Ballinger says it best: "Every generation demands a relevant demonstration of the Gospel of Jesus Christ." The challenge to us as the African American church is to be that relevant demonstration of the Gospel.

Casting the Vision

The word *vision* must be our framework for building a successful youth ministry that includes reaching junior and senior high school students. Perhaps the first question we must ask ourselves concerns how to measure success within the context of building an effective youth ministry. Luke 2:52 sets forth a brilliant model for which we should all strive. "And as Jesus continued to grow in body and mind, he grew also in the love of God and of those who knew Him" (PHILLIPS).

From this passage we can determine that our focus must

be broad in range of activities and specific in objectives, teaching our young people to love God and in turn making Him known. Within the text of Luke 2:52, we find a biblical base for building a successful youth ministry model. The ingredients in this model have been tested and proven to be very effective, not only in our church (Rosedale Park Baptist Church), but in hundreds of other churches throughout the United States and now in Kenya.

Before I go any further, a little background is in order. Several years ago I inherited the youth ministry from Pastor Gregory Alexander, who modeled and taught me the real message of Galatians 4:18 (PHILLIPS): "I will labor with you until Christ is formed in you." It is through his years of ministry, along with that of Pastor Haman Cross, Jr., that our success has been built.

Seasoned leaders. Before we examine issues of success, let's move immediately to review some key mistakes made by churches and Christian organizations as they work with young people. Quite often we place people in leadership with our children and youth who themselves are not seasoned in their walk with Christ. In some cases, it is not that they don't love the young people. They just have not arrived at a point of Christian maturity where they can be trusted with these impressionable minds. As a result, we find our young people being tossed around by every false doctrine.

The second element to this point is that we hear or read almost daily about youth workers gone amok or having abused teenagers. Today we live in a time when everybody just cannot be trusted with our most precious blessings. At Rosedale, every worker must complete our full new member's courses, after which they will spend the next year observing and working as ministry assistants. The only exception to this rule is if they are involved in a personal discipleship program with a pastor at Rosedale. Many ministries are moving toward state background checks.

Despite the obstacles, we still must find individuals who have a genuine love for God and for young people and who have a genuine desire to see young people grow in the fullness of Christ. Please don't just appoint someone to this ministry because of that person's availability or because he or she is young and "just loves having fun." (Later we will discuss in more detail the importance of making the right choices.)

Defining your ministry. The pastor and governing board must lay down a foundational definition of what the youth ministry is at your local church or organization. Defining who you are does not require you to give a complete breakdown of all you intend to do or accomplish. Defining simply allows you to understand why you exist. In many cases, you may use your church vision statement. Below you will find a universal statement I recommend to local groups and churches starting from scratch.

> Youth Ministry is ministering to young people in junior high and senior high school under the influence of the Holy Spirit within the context of the youth culture. Our goal is to help young people meet their felt needs from a biblical perspective.

What exactly does this mean? It means that the goal of the youth ministry is to help students learn to use a biblical grid to negotiate the various challenges and pressures placed on them. It is important for you to spell out the age range of students who are to be involved in your youth ministry. Years ago, the youth ministry was looked upon as dealing with everyone between the ages of one and thirty. If this is the pattern at your church (though not recommended), it is important that you make a conscious choice to divide your group by the already established school grades. Additionally, you might want to develop a statement of goals for each of those groups. In other words, the ministry to children can't be the same as the ministry devoted to reaching teenagers, given that each group faces different issues and problems. We just can't make youth ministry a catchall for every young person in our church or Christian organization.

Key ingredients. What are the key ingredients for building an on-fire, effective youth ministry? They are relevant Bible studies, missions, academic enhancement, sports, discipleship, evangelism, creative expression, local school outreach, special events, fellowship within the local assembly and with other Christian youth, and parental involvement.

The central ingredient for building a youth ministry that works is Bible study. It is important that workers learn to teach the Bible in a creative manner. The Bible is already relevant; we just need to enable our staff members to use teaching techniques that will allow them to contextualize Scripture so that the students can more easily relate to and understand it. Investing in the training of your youth workers will pay off in the end through growth in your students and of your church.

The definition statement talks about youth culture and biblical studies. We must help our students understand how to live within the youth culture through using the Bible as a basis for their decisions. That means helping our students to understand and respond to life's issues in the same way Christ would. *What would Jesus do?*

Relationships. Since we are in the vision process, it is important to use a multilevel approach. That requires your entire church to work in collaboration to meet the complete needs of the young people at your church or organization. Remember, we are in a war and are up against some of the finest technological advances of all time. In many cases, your ministry is competing against video games and television programs that have raised the consciousness of darkness to new levels. But in this war we offer something that video games, television, and other technological advances can't compete against—*relationships*. Every child has a need to belong and to experience *agape* love. That is exactly what we offer. When your church takes a collaborational approach to reaching teenagers, you will win every time!

It is important that every individual interacting with the young people from your congregation be of one accord regarding everything and that each department be in relationship with the other. For example, while the youth ministry is dealing with youth culture issues, the Sunday school department can be focusing on doctrinal and Bible knowledge that pertains to some of the same areas. If you have a youth choir,

choir leaders can be helping the students understand praise and worship while at the same time helping them to develop their own personal creative expressions of the Gospel message. *A ministry to youth requires relational departments and relational people.*

Developing Effective Programs

Now that you are involved in the *vision* process, it becomes important that your church begin to develop effective programs that help your students grasp vision and purpose. For instance, for the last eight years of my ministry I have lived this concept: *Students must live out the Great Commission and are capable of performing equally well many tasks generally attributed to adults.* The Bible says that the old will teach the young. This will only happen when you find students working side by side with the adult population of your church. This means that students should be actively involved in Bible studies, sports, creative expressions, evangelism, special events, and local school outreach. After you have started your ministry, your new goals must be teaching, equipping, and empowering the students to do the work of ministry (Ephesians 4:12).

Many churches fail to empower and equip their students to do ministry. Students want to be active in and involved with a true purpose-driven mission. At Rosedale, we see this lived out through various mission projects made available to high school students. It is our desire that every student actively involved in our ministry will participate in one local, one national, and one international mission project. Through this effort, we are casting a vision to our students regarding how they can be used by Christ in discharging the Great Commission. Furthermore, we are communicating that ministry is people reaching people for Christ with lifestyle and purpose.

Developing Leaders

Vision is a key component of a successful ministry. From my experience, vision will translate into the students' developing a strong sense of purpose for their individual lives. As we cast a vision and articulate a purpose, we need to keep in mind that our students need to see how they can have an impact in their spheres of influence. That will require that we develop special training in two areas: leadership development and evangelism. *Every student should know how to lead his or her friend to Christ.*

God requires us to develop young men and women who will lead His church in its charge to reclaim our cities and the lives of African Americans now affected by dysfunctional social policies and political leaders. In order for this to happen, we need leaders—men and women—who are willing to be sold out for the sake of Jesus Christ. Throughout the history of God's movement, we see men and women who had the foresight to invest in leadership development. Look at the wonderful relationship between Timothy and Paul, Moses and Joshua, Elijah and Elisha, and Naomi and Ruth, to name but a few. Effective youth ministry requires us to make leadership development a priority.

How do we select our future leaders? The first step is to observe your ministry and identify students who have a heart for other students. Often we look for the most articulate or the academic scholar. Those attributes are helpful, but God's first requirement is that we be *faithful, available,* and *teachable* (FAT). In many of our churches those who have these qualities may not be the very best students academically or the students with the most personality. They will be those who have demonstrated their faithfulness to the ministry and to God.

After you have located your FAT students, you have just found your first disciples. Here's a word of caution. Don't try to provide personal discipleship to a large number of students. Jesus was God, and He only chose twelve. If you have a large ministry and staff, make an effort to build small discipleship groups that will significantly enhance your students' growth. For some of you, the word *disciple* is too clergy oriented, and you might refer to the process as *mentoring.* Keep in mind the difference between the two. *Mentoring* is teaching the student everything you can. *Discipleship* is teaching and building a transparent relationship that allows the student to see your lifestyle in public and private. I strongly recommend discipleship!

How do we develop these leaders? It is quite simple. *Spend quality time with your students.* Jesus spent much of His time with His disciples and involved them in every aspect of His life. Following this model, in my circles everyone knows that it is not likely that you see me at any activity without one of the students I am currently discipling.

After you have cast the vision and have begun investing in the next generation of leaders, you will be ready to begin your program components. Most churches take the reverse procedure and by the time they are ready for leadership development, the students are twelfth graders and/or outside interests have grabbed their attention.

Developing Educational Enhancement Programs

Given the national urban education statistics, the African American church can no longer ignore this dilemma. Because of this crisis, we have an opportunity to create after-school learning programs. Volunteer staff from within your congregation and others can operate these programs. There are a number of foundations that will contribute to your ministry for the purpose of enhancing the academic performance of students in the neighborhood of your church.

Supporting Fellowship and Recreation

Every student, of course, enjoys great fellowship. Too often, we have been heavy-handed in fellowship and neglected the biblical component. A solid youth ministry will make every attempt to be balanced. It is very important that the students have an opportunity to interact with students from other churches or Christian organizations. They need to see that they are not alone in their quest to live for God. You might consider making every attempt to build relationships with churches in the neighborhood where most of your students attend school. This will be quite helpful as you attempt to expand your sphere of influence with your students. A word of caution: In your desire to create fellowship opportunities, be creative but don't compromise. Be careful not to fall into the pizza party syndrome. If those of us in youth ministry had a dime for every dollar we have invested in pizza, we would be very rich people.

Sports in the urban community is an incredible means for reaching teenagers and maintaining their attention. Recruit someone within your church who has a strong athletic interest to develop a sports ministry. Remember, just being a great athlete doesn't qualify someone to be a youth worker. Workers in this area must be trained. It is important that they understand that the mission of the ministry is producing Christ-centered lives. With the implementation of a sports program, you will find that your male and female students will become very enthusiastic. That enthusiasm will result in the students' inviting other students to be a part of your ministry. *Sports is a draw.*

The goal should always be to make your ministry exciting, creative, challenging, vision oriented and Christ centered. My former pastor during my elementary years was the Reverend Dr. William Carlton Audrey (former pastor of St. Paul A.M.E. Zion Church). He used to say regularly, "The growth of our church depends largely upon our youth." It is interesting that there probably is not much that I can quote from Dr. Audrey. Nevertheless, he made a lasting impression by casting the vision that if Christ's church is to continue its growth, we must invest in our youth. Perhaps today, my life vocation as a youth pastor can be attributed to the vision Dr. Audrey planted in my spirit over thirty-five years ago.

My advice to the reader: Cast the vision.

———————————

Dennis Talbert is youth pastor at Rosedale Park Baptist Church (Detroit) and director of Empower, a youth ministry.

Chapter 16

Never Give Up on Youth

BY EUGENE SEALS

We are now ready to hear the conclusion of the matter. Let me suggest that a couple of case studies are called for at this juncture. I have been where some readers are at this time. You may agree intellectually that youth ministry is good. But you may also have no intention of changing anything you are doing or not doing now. You are just the right sort of persons to read this chapter. Lots of today's adults bear testimony to the value of organized youth ministry. I am one of them, although the ministries I was blessed by had nothing of the organization and budget that are provided for today's youth. Our low- to no-budget, propless dramatic presentations were "countrified" by today's standards. Nonetheless, they left some impressions on me to this day. And they kept me off the street during an impressionable period of my life.

Changing Times

How times change! Twenty years after my own rather limited youth group experiences, my wife and I were unaware of the dynamics of the medium-sized church. (Our Laotian friend picked up on it right away. Phayrath declined to join our church because new members "had to teach Sunday school!")

Not being as astute as Phayrath, upon joining Calvary Mennonite (one hundred members strong), my wife and I became youth sponsors, and for three breathtaking years we sometimes single-handedly took our truly extraordinary youth group (and other youth groups on occasion) to Lake Elsinore (Southern California), Tijuana (Mexico), Mesa Verde and Phoenix (Arizona), and Calvin College (Grand Rapids). We camped overnight to join the good-natured excitement of the Rose Parade and went "to the snow" at Big Bear (mountainous area near San Bernardino) as only semitropical people can do. And we went to Disneyland when Disney was "cool."

Further, our near off-Broadway caliber youth performed the *Come Together* musical after it became so popular. We "retreated" at a Pacific Palisades campground to advance more earnestly toward the mark of the prize of the high calling in Jesus. Our youth conducted vacation Bible school in historic Allensworth (California) and did street ministry from time to time in Los Angeles. Of course, we had the obligatory car wash/bake sales, which our group converted to another witnessing opportunity.

Our job was to make friends for the Gospel. So it is the same around the globe, as we learned in Venezuela. Partly because of these experiences, many of our youth grew up to become responsible parents, working men and women, church college students, fashion models, attorneys, church leaders, and good, decent human beings.

Work-in-Process

My coeditor, Matthew Parker, tells me how influential youth workers and others were in his life. To get a fuller appreciation of their impact, let's go back to his beginning.

On November 14, 1945, Matthew Parker was born in

Cincinnati to Matt and Ruth Parker. A year later, Mr. Matt Parker secured a good job in Detroit's booming post-war auto industry, causing the family to relocate to the Motor City. Like thousands of other African American parents before and since (including my own), the Parkers made a home for themselves and their effervescent little son in Detroit's Black Bottom, a near–East Side ghetto.

Before the younger Parker was four years old, his mother died, leaving his father to raise two sons. In the best African American tradition of the day, the senior Parker committed himself to doing "whatever it takes to raise [his] two boys."

When Matthew finished high school, he was unable to gain admission to a state university. So he enrolled in a junior college, where he was heavily involved in cross-country. While a student there, Matthew was arrested for theft, after which he returned to Detroit and later worked on Chrysler's assembly line.

Several years later, in 1966, Matthew enrolled in Grand Rapids School of Bible and Music (GRSBM)—one of only two African American students. While a student there, he had two life-altering experiences. The first was a spiritual encounter that led him to commit his life to Christ. The second was a "where the rubber meets the road" confrontation with racism as practiced by white evangelical teachers and leaders. His experience was similar to that of so many other African American Christians who report their shock and disillusionment that so many white Christians stood in the doorway of the church, metaphorically speaking, in an ill-fated attempt to keep blacks from gaining full access. Unfortunately, I have heard Dr. A. Charles Ware tell of blacks who have let the adversary succeed in that effort, with literally disastrous consequences. Such is the paradox of life in the African Diaspora (those scattered for reasons of slavery and, more recently, for emigration).

It was hard for Matthew to understand why Jesus Christ would sacrifice His life for a person such as Matthew and ask nothing in return. It was even more perplexing why other children of the King would have such a hard time extending proper consideration to African American Christians as people for whom Christ died. These experiences would have a far-reaching impact on Matthew's life and ministry. Rather than making him *bitter*, however, he became *better* as a result of what he suffered.

While at GRSBM, Matthew had the opportunity to hear and meet Tom Skinner, a noted evangelist and speaker. Matthew is fond of telling how the best leaders accomplish goals without making people feel they have been led. In the spring of 1969, Skinner took Parker aside, spent time and money on him, and encouraged him to grow as a leader. Skinner became a mentor to Parker from that point forward, as was his practice on various college campuses. There are many leaders today in the fields of missions, leadership development, pastoring, publishing, and more who owe their inspiration to Skinner's mentoring. Skinner practiced many of the same principles promoted by Parker, including networking and encouraging African American–led ministries.

Matthew went on to complete a diploma at GRSBM, a B.A. at Wheaton College, and an M.A. at University of Detroit—not bad for an at-risk kid from Detroit's Black Bottom, as he might say. Excelling in cross-country and track, Matthew was invited to compete internationally with Overseas Crusades Ministries. During these trips, Matthew experienced the unusual feeling of affirmation from citizens of other nationalities. The boost to his self-esteem contributes, no doubt, to his feeling at ease as he converses with presidents and popes as well as with common persons such as myself.

While working on his bachelor's degree, Matthew served as Minority Student Advisor at Wheaton. His contributions there included developing community resources for students, contacts for summer mission opportunities for minority students, and creation of the Student Organization for Urban Leadership. Implementing such projects enabled Matthew to develop his administrative skills, drawing on the expertise of college administrators and staff.

Administration and Innovation

After two years as administrator at J. Allen Caldwell Private Schools, Matthew established the Urban Ministry Program at William Tyndale College in Farmington Hills, Michigan. Never one to accept unworkable, timeworn constraints, Matthew introduced such innovations as holding evening courses in community churches in Detroit, thereby placing classes fifteen to twenty miles closer to a whole new market of urban students. In addition, Matthew's securing of accreditation for the Urban Studies Program led to accreditation of the entire college. As the program flourished and operated with a net positive income, Matthew was appointed Associate Vice President in 1985, where he served until 1988.

While at Tyndale, Matthew created three institutes: the Institute for Urban Youth Ministry, the Institute for Hispanic Studies, and the Institute for Muslim Studies.

Parker also observed that African American graduates of Bible colleges were consistently overlooked by white evangelical organizations as viable candidates for the positions for which the students had trained. As a result, the Center for Black Church Development was established. This Center employed black graduates of William Tyndale's Urban Studies Program, thus utilizing and further developing the skills of leaders of the future.

Matthew played an instrumental role in founding the Hamilton Avenue Missionary Baptist Church when a white suburban church discontinued its Sunday school busing ministry's outreach to inner city Detroit. The suburban church was willing to provide initial funding for Detroit Afro-American Mission to begin a church planting project. Matthew initially acted as consultant on the project, which moved from a vacation Bible school to a Sunday school to a Sunday morning service to hiring a pastor. Later, Parker assumed interim pastoral responsibilities in the congregation after the first pastor was dismissed.

National and International Intersections

In 1984, he planned and directed the National Summit on Black Church Development. A second summit was held in 1986, a third in 1990, with subsequent meetings in 1992, 1994, and 1996.

Never one to let grass grow under his feet, Matthew joined a group of leaders who organized Atlanta 88: The Congress on Evangelizing Black America. This was in response to the exclusion of African Americans from the agenda of the 1985 Conference on Evangelizing Ethnic America. Matthew served as chair. The Conference was noted for its gathering of African American Christians from diverse backgrounds. Not intending to create a competitive institution with a private agenda, the steering committee dissolved the Atlanta 88 corporation following the conference.

In 1986, John Perkins introduced Matthew to a group of church leaders who subsequently met with President Reagan and Vice President Bush. They were known as the Religious Alliance Against Pornography (RAAP). As a member of the RAAP executive committee, Matthew was particularly influential in gaining support for greater representation of minorities and women in the Alliance's executive and steering committees. Matthew was among RAAP members greeted by Pope John Paul II during a 1992 meeting with Vatican representatives to plan an international antipornography conference.

Institute for Black Family Development

In response to the 1986 Bill Moyers documentary, "The Vanishing Black Family: A Crisis in Black America," the Institute for Black Family Development was formed in 1987. Matthew played a key role in founding the Institute, which was designed to be a national Christian consulting agency providing leadership training for pastors, their wives, and youth leaders. With assistance from Prison Fellowship, Focus on the Family, and World Vision, Matthew became the Institute's first president, a post he continues to hold.

Above all, Matthew has a driving passion to give back to the community, especially to the youth. He knows the value of unplanned, unorganized interaction with young people. His uncle helped him get his head together after that humiliating arrest in the late sixties. Matthew feels we should always be ready to pour ourselves into a young person's life, particularly if the individual is from a single-parent home.

On an organized level, Matthew is in his fifth year of mentoring twenty-three young people, whom he affectionately dubs the Generals, challenging them to excel by virtue of the very name of the group. He committed to them that he is going to be involved in their lives until he dies. This is one fruit of Tom Skinner's mentoring Matthew as a young man.

Spiritual Parents

There were other influences, too. After losing both parents early in life, Matthew asked Barbara Walton and Lloyd Blue to be his spiritual parents. "They have both been very instrumental in shaping the decisions I have made in my life," Matthew explains. "They allowed me to watch them—to see them with their spouses and children, with their friends, in their ministries. . . . Their investment in me, I am now passing on to others." Matthew appreciates how much his spiritual dad and mom helped him to understand that God has to be first in a person's life. They told him that anything—attitude, event, person, or whatever—that caused him to focus on that thing, rather than on God, is idolatry. This is one of the reasons Matthew will not allow any racist person to cause him to hate or experience frustration.

Matthew's diverse involvements have included serving as a consultant to a variety of ministries and projects, ranging from Mendenhall Ministries and Oakdale Fellowship Church to Christianity Today, Detroit Youth for Christ, and World Vision. He has applied his administrative skills to business in the production of a film, *The Black American Family: A Christian Legacy*, and publication and coediting of several books, including *Called to Lead: Wisdom for the Next Generation of African American Leaders*, *Black Church Development*, *Man to Man*, and *Woman to Woman*.

Matthew operated his own publishing company for a period of time. Matthew's skills and contributions have been recognized through numerous awards, including the following:

Achievement Award and Minority Student Award (Wheaton College, 1974)

Men of Achievement

Outstanding Young Men of America (1980 and 1981)

Who's Who Among Black Americans (1986)

Mission Leadership Award (Destiny 87)

Urban Leadership Development Citation (American Biographical Institute, 1987)

Men of Achievement Citation (International Biographical
Centre, Cambridge, England, 1988)

Leadership Award (National Black Evangelical Association, 1988)

Matthew married his wife, Karon, in 1980. They have
three sons and two daughters. The children are being home-
schooled by Karon.

Fruit

This book has attempted to present ideas on ministering
to the next generation. Our patient, joyful, sometimes frustrating labors will be amply rewarded by the God who promised
that His Word will not return to Him void, but will result in the
nurturing and development of the young Monique Brewers, the
Deshawn Muldrows, the Michael Ealys, and the Ebony Parkers
of today into another internationally respected Matthew Parker
or another locally loved Yalonda Dixon.

There is no premium on achieving an international profile.
Achievement in the world's terms is not the point—although
we encourage people to be all God created them to be. The goal
is for the maturing young person to use all his or her gifts to the
glory of God. The Lord is looking for a few good men and
women to provide the love and mentoring which are the soil
from which the leaders of tomorrow will emerge.

*Eugene Seals is executive editor for Quality Publishing Systems
(Farmington Hills, Mich.) and teaches at Spring Arbor College
(Mich.).*

Be Sure to Read All the Other Books in the NEW Lift Every Voice Imprint

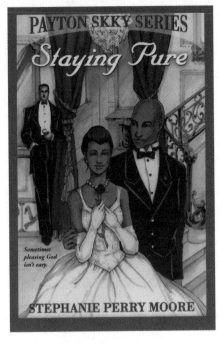

Staying Pure

Staying Pure addresses the pressures African-American girls face to stay physically pure and remain devoted to God. Not only is Payton Skky popular, but she is also dating the best looking guy at her high school. While he is pressuring her to sleep with him, Payton is content to wait, convinced that he is the one she will marry. As the pressure increases Payton starts to wonder if waiting is really worth it, especially since she believes that they will always be together. If she had sleeps with him will they be together forever? Payton struggles with these questions and with exactly what is God's plan for and meaning of purity.

Quality Paperback 0-8024-4236-6

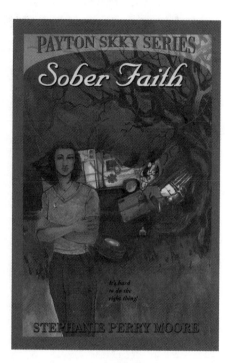

Sober Faith

Payton Skky has gotten over her ex-boyfriend and is now dating a strong Christian, Tad, who   is keeping her accountable. Her friends, however, are still struggling with their identity and exactly what is right and wrong. Chasing after fun they discover alcohol and drugs. They spend time experimenting without thinking of the consequences. Payton wants to help her friends realize the dangers in what they are doing, but she also wants to be accepted by them. Can she do both? How far is too far? What about Tad, who doesn't approve of what Payton's friends are doing? Can she help her friends without compromising her faith?

Quality Paperback 0-8024-4237-4

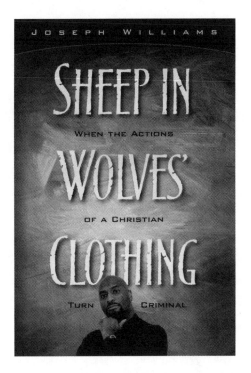

Sheep in Wolves' Clothing
When the Actions of a Christian Turn Criminal

A heroin addict. A career criminal. How did Joseph Williams walk through the valley of the shadow of death and emerge not only safe, but reconciled to and on fire for Jesus Christ?

Read the amazing and inspiring story of how Williams was a lost sheep who was doggedly pursued by a loving Savior he had invited into his heart as a teen. Be encouraged as you pray for the lost sheep in your life or as you contemplate returning to the fold of the loving Shepherd.

Quality Paperback 0-8024-6594-3